RESTLESS

DISPATCHES FROM A
LIFETIME OF ADVENTURE

JOHN PECK

WITH GEORGE BULL

Praise

"John Peck is not only an adventurer but a skilful and beguiling writer. This book is more than an interesting biography – it is funny, reflective, wise and, above all, inspirational."

Adrian Furnham, Professor of Psychology at University College London and **Sunday Times** *columnist*

"I would say that John Peck is in the same league as the explorer Robin Hanbury Tenison. He is undoubtedly a leader with that rare ability to inspire others. I was particularly taken with his address to the police college in which he defines good leadership as the ability to know your men."

Captain Peter Voute CBE, Royal Navy

"If I was in quicksand and I could call one person, it would be John Peck. He can look into your eyes, assess what's there and help you take on what at first appears impossible."

Alex Mahon, former CEO of Shine Group, now CEO at The Foundry

"This fascinating book by John Peck describes how his thirst for adventure shaped not only his character but the whole pattern of his life. Many of his adventures were first time experiences rather the culmination of years of training. They were undertaken because his instinct was to pursue each idea when it arose rather than abandon it.

This is the true spirit of an adventurer and he obviously revelled in it. The stories themselves are riveting. Physical fitness, determination, expedition planning and stresses on family life are all dealt with and collectively offer sound advice for any would be adventurers thinking of following in his footsteps."

Major-General Ian Freer CB CBE

"*Restless* is a refreshingly honest "warts and all" reflection based on hard-learnt experience. If you have ever had great ambition but perhaps lacked the courage to go for it or wondered whether the risk is worth it, then this book is for you."

Alan Hooper, Founding Director,
Centre for Leadership Studies, University of Exeter

"The words 'no' and 'impossible' are sidelined in John's unending pursuit of the next adventure."

Emy Rumble-Mettle, Director, Talent & Development, GroupM

"This is a read that will appeal to all ages. For the young, it will be inspirational – if you have the courage and the determination you can achieve anything you want. For the more mature, it will generate feelings of, 'God, I wish I had done something like that.'"

John Purnell GM QPM DL, Former Deputy Assistant Commissioner
Metropolitan Police and currently Deputy Lieutenant of Greater London

"I first met John some years back while taking part in a Bravehearts program he was running in the remote islands off Scotland's coast.

He articulated to some degree his experiences back then but his focus on us as his participants made him withhold all the nuggets that I have been fortunate enough to collect from his book! I am grateful to have read the book but blessed to have met the man."

Karl Lokko, former gang leader turned community worker campaigning to reform gang culture in the UK

"*Restless* is a compelling and passionate reflection on a life well lived. Peck's desire to explore his physical and mental limit is equal parts thrilling and inspiring. It made me long to go on more adventures of my own."

Rick Pearson, Editor, **Men's Running**

"John is a quiet spoken, affable man, thoughtful and rational; a surface demeanour, however, that masks a passionate core of molten steel and a determination to do the right thing in the right way. One example of this out of many I could chose from, hinted at by him here, was at a time of dangerous tensions with volatile communities in London... John steered paths between successfully meeting the expectations of a divided diverse society, vocal activists and difficult politicians in mountainous political seas... How he achieved that is revealed in his stories of other kinds of mountains and mountainous seas. No wonder he was a great police officer in the most diverse, problem-riddled, capital city on earth."

John Grieve CBE QPM, former Deputy Commissioner Metropolitan Police and Professor Emeritus London Metropolitan University

"God only knows what has driven John on all these hare-brained, frankly barmy adventures, but I'm supremely envious of his drive, his focus and his good humour throughout. This book compacts decades of lunatic but ultimately life-affirming capers into a barnstorming read. If I turn out to be half the man he is (and my time's running out!), I'll be very happy."

Rob da Bank, BBC Radio 1 DJ
and co-founder of music festival, Bestival

"I have, on a cold winter's evening, been transported to far-away mountains to climb with John, to run on scorched earth with him, overcome mountainous seas as I rowed with him, taken to the pinnacle of pain and utter exhaustion... I have been elevated, humbled and challenged... I have traversed the globe with him – and all of this while sitting at home with my dog asleep at my feet."

David Kay, retired international marketing and
aviation consultant to the film industry

For Elaine, who has been my rock and my mental
base camp through many an adventure.

You have my love forever.

Contents

"The mountains are the means; the man is the end.
The idea is to improve the man,
not to reach the top of the mountains."
Walter Bonatti

Foreword

This is a book that will, if you're like me, grip your attention and take you on a distinctly white knuckle ride from time to time. One aspect of literature vital to me is that I am lifted, ideally within a paragraph, to the scene of the action. John Peck, our restless author whom I met many years ago, does just that.

John made me feel that I was leaping to safety over the rail of his yacht *Chayka of Ardour* as the Yarmouth lifeboat swept up beside her on the next wave in that storm in 1975. I climbed the Matterhorn with him, I rowed the Atlantic and travelled to Africa and to the Arctic. His descriptions are vivid, his language real, straightforward and credible.

To my mind, having lived within the world of mountain exploration for over half a century, today it often seems to me that endeavour and adventure have tended to become publicity stunts, driven by media attention, by a relentless public relations team and, if one pauses to investigate, the dramas are not infrequently faked or exaggerated – and, we learn from the grapevine, well-paid. You will find nothing like this here. John tells it as it is, as he dreamt it, found out how do it, and carried it off.

John has also "done time" – and not behind bars. He has served his country. He has a distinguished record of public service, in the armed forces and in the police force. Few combine that sense of duty and dedication with a wild side that has taken John, and his friends, to their distinct limits.

You may be breathless, incredulous, wondrous, and often worried at why John simply did not rest, and why, having taken such risks early in life he did not settle, as many do. That is perhaps his magic.

Eric Shipton wrote in the 1940s in *Upon That Mountain*: "There are few treasures of more lasting worth than the experience of a way of life that is in itself wholly satisfying. Such, after all, are the only possessions of which no fate, no cosmic catastrophe can deprive us; nothing can alter the fact, if for one moment in eternity, however brief, we have really lived."

In *Restless*, John tells us all how *he* has really lived, and as you read this book, he'll take you on journeys you'll never forget.

Dr Charles Clarke

Neurologist, mountaineering doctor and yachtsman
Kishtwar, Kashmir 1965-1974; Everest SW Face 1975 and NE Ridge 1982; Kongur
1981; Menlungtse 1988; Sepu Kangri & Eastern Tibet 1996-2000.
Skipper: *Whisky Galore* – Three Peaks Yacht Race 2009, 2010, 2011.

Introduction

I started climbing for reasons that it took me a long time to understand. It was addictive, sure, but it wasn't about adrenalin. The prolonged physical pain, the financial commitment, the drain on loved ones' patience, the months of planning and the glory of peak bagging were all too fleeting for that. More often than not, expeditions to far-flung places came down to hard work. Nor was it about being the best climber. With a busy life running a police station, a marriage and three young sons, and having never been particularly competitive, my technical skills as a climber hit competent and stayed that way. And I was happy with that. But what climbing, and later sailing, running and rowing, gave me was the chance to test myself – and usually in good company.

People who know me sometimes wonder aloud how I've had time to fill my life with adventures. I usually tell them it's about getting to the point of no return, where you are committed to making something happen. But it's also more than that. At times, I am simply compelled to do it. Climber Mo Anthoine puts it best. In Al Alvarez's seminal profile of him, Anthoine calls his motivation "feeding the rat" (also the title of his book). You might think of yourself as a pretty slick bloke, he says, but until you test yourself, you'll never know how big the gap is between who you think you are and who you really are.

The need to feed the rat that gnaws inside me has led me to the top of mountains, across baking deserts and Arctic ice, and has even propelled me across an ocean. All of this would test not only my own limits, but also those of the people closest to me, and I would come to understand the price that must be paid for a life of adventure. I would also learn how to translate the things that I learnt in the crucible of these experiences so that I could pass them on to other people in a way that would help them to make sense of their own lives. But all of that would come later.

This little book is a collection of accounts of those adventures. It is partly a way of thanking those people who have had the courage to travel with me on this journey, while also, I hope, providing a source of inspiration for those dreaming about starting their own. What are you waiting for?

J.P.
The Dukes

ONE
Southpaw

When I was eight years old, I went to the cinema with my parents to see Tarzan. I was so excited by it that as soon as I got home that afternoon, I rushed out into the garden and raced to the top of my favourite tree. I decided to try something that I'd never had the courage to do, and I leapt from one high branch towards another. Unfortunately, my hands were too small and weren't strong enough to grip the branch that I was aiming for; I plummeted to the ground, landing with a hefty thud on the grass below.

I can clearly remember the thrill of adrenalin as I lay on the ground, winded, but exulted to still be in one piece. I never told my parents, and it seems ridiculous to think it now, but I knew that in some strange way my life had been transformed in that moment. I suddenly felt years older. It was the first of many such moments where I would begin to understand the feelings that awaited me when I pushed at the edges of myself.

As a boy, Sunday mornings would often be an opportunity to spend time with my father. My sisters and I would climb into my parents' bed and he would tell us stories about his life. He had grown

3

up in the colonial days of Shanghai, gone on to become a young policeman in London during the Blitz and then later, halfway through the war, joined the RAF to become a fighter pilot. I vowed then that when I grew up, I would also have adventurous tales to tell.

In my grandfather's house, I found a book called *Heroes of Modern Adventure* and I would study in awe its tales of the explorers of the 19th and early 20th centuries who had trodden paths where no one had ever been before – the icy cold world of Antarctica, or the African jungle, where the canopy was so dense and the air so thick with humidity a man could lose his mind.

I lived in awe of the adventurers that I read about. Men and women who had given up the relative comfort and luxury of large Victorian houses to venture forth into wilderness; places that were simply a name on a map. Theirs was a quest to explore these vast unknown spaces and, perhaps for many of them, themselves. I vowed that one day, I would make this adventurous life happen for myself. But to have even suggested it then would have invited ridicule.

Growing up, I was the very opposite of these so-called heroes. With two strong-willed elder sisters and an even more strong-willed mother, I was a timid child – self-effacing, often embarrassed and lonely. By the time I was seven years old, my father had decided that I needed "toughening up" and that boarding school would be the appropriate place for that. Having tried to get me a place at Solihull Public School in Edgbaston where he and his brother had gone to, he was told I would have to wait for a year for a place to become available, but, in the meantime, I could attend the prep school as a day boy. My father thought this was a good idea and sent me to live with my grandparents nearby in Birmingham.

As far as I was concerned, it was a terrible decision. I was regularly bullied at school and hadn't a clue how to stand up for myself. I should have found respite with my grandparents, but instead I found my grandmother to be something of an ogre; scarier even than the rumours of a ghost that inhabited the dark recesses of her house. I lived in dread of climbing the gnarled old staircase to the third floor attic room, where I slept fitfully in fear of floorboards that creaked in the middle of the night, counting down the weeks until I got to see my parents again. "What kind of start in life was this for a would-be adventurer?" I thought.

— • —

With my year at prep school out of the way, I found myself in a dormitory of 12 other boys, and from there on in, things would get worse before they got better. When my parents visited me a few weeks into my first term, they were shocked at my tears and pleas to take me home. But my father's solution, which seemed unsentimental at the time, would eventually prove to be one of the best decisions that he ever made for me: he enrolled me in boxing classes.

My time in the ring was alarming. The sting of being routinely hit on the nose, of being unable to get out of the way, let alone counter, was an assault on my senses. For weeks, every session was the same, the shock never lessening; sent reeling into the ropes. But since I had no choice but to persevere, eventually, it all changed: I learned to dance in the ring. I was taught how to duck and weave, to dodge punches, while making sure mine truly connected and, as a 'southpaw' – a left-handed boxer – I became skilled at catching people off guard.

From then on, things didn't just change for me in the ring, but outside it too. It is an unfortunate fact of life that it is often only once people know that you are capable of hitting them, and that you are not afraid to do so, that they will leave you alone.

Freed from the bullies, in time, life at Solihull Public School became more fun than living at home in the school holidays. My father was often absent with his job in the police force and my mother spent a lot of her time resentful and angry as a result. As the summers passed, the more I longed to get away and spread my wings. The awe that I held for those past heroes of modern adventure had never dimmed – if anything, that candle burned even brighter. Like a lot of boys my age, no doubt, I had a poster of Mount Everest on my bedroom wall and spent hours gazing up at it, transported.

— • —

A week-long outward bound course to Towyn on the coast of North Wales when I was 17 years old did much to reinforce my desire for the outdoor life. The winter months in Towyn do not suffer fools gladly and neither did the army NCOs responsible for us. Every morning, we would be woken at seven o'clock and made to run over the sand dunes to the sea, where we would have to plunge into the icy water and stay there until we were told to get out and run back to the barracks.

Our final exercise that week was on the foothills of Mount Snowdon. We had camped out in the snow and been woken early in the morning by the course leaders telling us that a climber had gone missing and that we had 10 minutes to get ready to go out on a search and rescue. With no clue that this was simply a routine exercise, all of us were swept up in the drama. Carrying heavy rucksacks, and with boots soaked through, we struggled on in knee-deep snow for hours in search of our missing climber. I had never felt so exhausted and, as I kept pushing on, I tasted for the first time the secret knowledge that you are pushing yourself right to the outer edges of your capability.

From that moment on, I was eager to get out into the mountains at every opportunity. That same summer, my cousin Richard, who was a year older than me, had recently passed his driving test and I persuaded him to drive us up to North Wales in his old MG TD sports car.

We found our way to Llanberis, a small village at the base of Snowdon and home to the famous sports shop of renowned rock climber Joe Brown. We bought a brand new rope, two slings, a climbing harness each and a couple of things called "nuts", which we were told could be jammed into cracks to secure us to the rock while we were "belaying". It was all new to us but, flush with excitement, we figured that we would get the hang of it. Armed with our rudimentary kit and a climbing guide book, we set off for Llanberis Pass.

We pitched our tent in the valley and looked up at the routes that we had come to climb – all of them with fantastic names such as "Cemetery Gates" or "Flying Buttress". The easiest route that we could find in the area was graded "very difficult", so it was with some trepidation that we made our way to its start and I set off to lead us up.

All of my fears dissolved as I climbed effortlessly up that first pitch. My body fell quickly into a rhythm with the rock and I felt what climbers describe as being "in flow". My focus was calm and absolute; all of my energy directed at that moment. It was an exquisite feeling.

Pitch by pitch, Richard and I made our way up our first climb in the Llanberis Pass, eventually topping out and making our way to the head of the Pen Y Gwryd valley where we knew there was a pub. Inside, everywhere the walls were bedecked with old photos of famous climbers and bits of kit. I felt exhilarated that climbing had proved to be everything that I had dreamed of and, as we stood there with our pints of beer, we felt like we were peering into an adult world that was finally opening up to us.

— • —

Although I had conquered my initial unhappiness at Solihull and, despite the promise of a public school education, by 18 I had dropped out to take up an offer of work at an estate agents in the town where my parents lived. It had been suggested that I'd make partner in time and I was meant to be doing a correspondence course with the Chartered Institute of Surveyors – but I was bored to death and still desperate to get out and see the world.

At home one evening, my father, who had noticed that I hadn't been doing my work, asked me what the matter was. I showed him a newspaper cutting with an advert for applicants to join the Navy's fleet air arm as helicopter pilots. Rather than give me a dressing down as I expected, he said simply: "Well, what have you done about it then?" I felt a huge weight lift off my shoulders and the next morning set off to apply.

I was accepted for an extended, three-day interview fairly quickly, but my optimism would be short-lived. I lasted half a day before I was sent packing as a failure.

"If you'd like to apply to be a naval officer, we can talk again," I was told, "but you'll never make a helicopter pilot. Your coordination is useless."

Since helicopters were expensive bits of kit, the Navy couldn't afford to lose one by putting me at the controls. I went home with my tail between my legs, despondent and embarrassed.

It was my father who picked up the pieces. Though he could be stubborn and unsentimental, he was, above all, a great fatalist. He told me not to worry, that although we couldn't always understand why at the time, things usually turned out for the best. Since I seemed so keen to adopt service life, he suggested that I applied to become an army officer with the local Staffordshire Regiment instead. I followed his advice and was granted an extended interview by the regular commissions board. I made it through the full three days this time – but again I was told that I hadn't passed. They told me they thought I would pass next time, however, so why didn't I become a soldier for a year to prove myself? Then, they'd look at the reports from my regiment and make a decision on whether I really was officer material.

I gladly took the advice. From the sleepy Stafford town where I had once stacked files in an estate agents, finally a new world of possibility was opening up to me.

— • —

On the day that I arrived at the Staffordshire barracks, I had been a public-school boarder for 10 years. In many ways, I couldn't have been more different to the 20 lads I was to share barracks with, many of whom had quite checkered pasts. But boarding school had taught me how to keep my head down and survive. I was as fit as they were and the boxing lessons from school came in handy, so after a couple of early scraps in the barracks room, I didn't get any trouble again. Besides, before long, they had stolen most of my possessions – which meant we were quickly all on a level playing field.

I avoided them if they ever got really drunk in town, as that would invariably end up with someone getting arrested, but mostly I just did what they did. If I am going to be an officer, I ought to use the time to understand the way these lads think, I said to myself. I also listened very carefully to what they'd say about all the various officers assigned to us while we were in the depot barracks.

Often officers would rotate, staying on for only a short time to look after us. Some of them the soldiers would hate from the word go, while others they just couldn't respect; but every now and then, one officer would really get it right. It was these guys that I was most interested in. I'd look at them and think, 'What is it this guy's doing?'

One of these officers was Jenkins. The soldiers loved him and, as he knew I was coming up, he decided to take me under his wing. One day, towards the end of my year at the barracks, he took me to one side and told me that very soon I was going to be called for an interview with the colonel of the regiment, and he'd be the one who decided whether or not I was ready to start officer training. Could he give me some advice from his own interview? Of course, I said, eager to know everything I could to pass.

Jenkins had turned up for his interview to find this Colonel Blimp-type character sitting behind the desk: "Right Jenkins, come in and sit down," he'd said. He'd looked at Jenkins, looked down at his papers. "I've been reading about you, Jenkins. What I want to know is, have you got any foibles?"

"No, sir! I haven't got any foibles, sir." replied Jenkins.

Unconvinced, the Colonel replied, "Well, are you a piss artist, Jenkins?"

"No, sir! I mean, I like a glass of beer, but no sir, I wouldn't call myself a piss artist."

This time, the Colonel asked if he was a crumpet man.

"Girls, sir? Well no, I wouldn't call myself a crumpet man, sir. I have the occasional girlfriend… a companion, sir," Jenkins replied.

By this point apparently, the Colonel was looking dismayed.

"Oh. Well have you got a dawg, then?" he said.

"I beg your pardon, have I got a what, sir?"

"You know, a dawg, a dawg, Jenkins."

"Oh, a dog! No, sir, I haven't got a dog… a dawg, sir."

The Colonel leaned in: "So you're telling me, Jenkins, that you haven't got any foibles at all?"

"No sir!"

"Well fucking well get some then! Otherwise, Jenkins, you will go through this man's army, for three years or whatever it is, you will come and you will go, and, one day, people will say, 'Jenkins? Jenkins? Who the fucking hell was Jenkins?'"

Jenkins, it turned out, had taken the Colonel's advice quite literally: if the soldiers were staying up late, getting pissed, he was right there with them – and he had a great black Labrador that used to follow him everywhere. So, sure enough, when it eventually came time for my officer's interview, the first thing I did was get myself a *dawg*.

TWO

The Smoking Mountain

The great Eric Shipton once said that if an expedition couldn't be planned on the back of a fag packet, then it wasn't worth doing. As a restless young army officer on border patrols in Belize in 1966, I found it was just that kind of minimalist approach that would lead me to climb my first big peak: Mexico's Mount Popocatépetl.

The plan was simple: a fellow officer, Hedley Robinson, and I would hitchhike our way to San Salvador and then on, through bandit country, to Mexico City. Once there, we would track down a group of mountain rescue climbers that we'd heard about called Sorrocco Alpino and persuade them to take us up the mountain. But at 17,802 feet, Popocatépetl was to be no small undertaking and we would need to train – the problem was, where? Other than some low mountains to the south, Belize is essentially flat and in Belize City, the only thing of any height for miles around was a 300-foot radio mast. One quiet afternoon on patrol, we looked up at the radio mast through the midday haze and decided that it would have to do.

I felt that if we were going to go to the trouble of getting up there, we should at least leave our mark. We sewed together two white army bed sheets to make a flag and, with red paint, wrote in big letters, "How does this grab you, darlin'?", the title of Nancy Sinatra's big hit at the time.

Having made some discreet enquiries with a girl who worked at the radio station, Hedley had heard that it closed down in the evenings and, therefore, the radio mast would have no electricity going through it. That was good enough for us and, one night, we set off in dark clothes and balaclavas to cut our way through the perimeter fence. To our joy, there were no guard dogs and we were soon looking up at a box-like structure about 18 inches square, supported by taut, thick wires that rose and rose until they disappeared into the sky.

We were keen to make sure that what the girl at the radio station had said was true, so Hedley licked a piece of grass and touched it to the metal framework to see if it tingled. A big spark instantly shot out, which wasn't too encouraging. We decided to move to plan B. This meant leaping onto the structure without any other part of us touching the ground. We tossed a coin for it and Hedley reluctantly agreed to be the first to try.

He leapt on and, much to our relief and amazement, he didn't fry. I followed suit and we made our way up, like Jack up the giant beanstalk, to the top of the 300-foot antenna, holding on tight as we swayed wildly in the night breeze. Hedley unfurled our homemade flag, which caught the wind beautifully and, having secured it, we clambered back down to the safety of the officer's mess and two large gin and tonics.

The next day, the Belizean Prime Minister and the British governor

14

were driving through the city and, to their horror, saw our flag flying proudly from the mast. We later heard that the Prime Minister allegedly believed that terrorists had planted the flag as a direct affront to him. He issued instructions that it should be removed immediately, but nobody would go up and take it down – even after a $50 reward was offered to any climber plucky enough to go and remove it. When the flag was eventually removed some days later, it did not take much forensic examination to reveal that it was made of two army bed sheets. Fortunately, I had already briefed our friendly quartermaster and he had reported the theft of two white sheets from the barrack's washing line to the local police two days before. But things were hotting up and I was starting to get nervous.

Our commanding officer was treating us suspiciously and it wasn't long before we were hauled in.

"If what I imagine happened is true," he said, "you had better own up and go apologise to the PM."

Having taken the hint, we paraded into the PM's office and apologised for having put our flag on his pole. He seemed so relieved to hear that it was us, and not the terrorists that he had originally suspected, that he let the matter drop. It wasn't until a few months later, while delivering a diplomatic bag to San Salvador, that I found out that the incident had set alarm bells ringing in the British Embassy and that they had been on the brink of declaring a state of emergency. This was all the more embarrassing given that we were supposed to be on a peacekeeping mission.

I seemed to develop a bit of a fetish for flags around this time. When I was posted in Berlin six months later, I spotted a Union Jack flying from the top of one of the highest buildings in the city. Under the cover of darkness, I led a small team past the guards on duty and we neatly removed the flag and hung it on a flagpole outside the guardroom of the American Army base – much to everyone's surprise when they saw it the following morning.

— • —

While Hedley and my opportunities to train at any sort of altitude had dwindled after the fiasco with the radio mast, our enthusiasm for climbing Popocatépetl had not. After two or three days hitching lifts with lorry drivers on the road from Belize, we eventually made it to Mexico City and the welcoming arms of the Sorrocco Alpino. They proved to be a generous and hospitable bunch and, though we spoke no Spanish and they no English, we got on like a house on fire and this was soon to become a joint British/Mexican attempt on the mountain.

Popocatépetl literally means "Smoking Mountain" and it is a volcano that is still active to this day. Having been forced to back off on our first attempt by severe weather, it was starting to dawn on us that this would be a serious undertaking. We resolved to try again with what's generally known as an "alpine start" – leaving the hut at the base of the mountain at four o'clock in the morning. It was a decision that served us well, as the snow was still frozen, allowing us the luxury of solid ground rather than the knee-deep slush you get when the sun warms the mountain face. But if the snow was solid, the ice face was rock-hard and it was easy to see how so many people had died on what the locals often called "Killer Mountain".

After four hours, we made it to the final approach to the crest of the volcano. It was now that our Mexican partners suggested that we rope together before attempting the most exposed section. Something about the decision seemed clumsy and Hedley, who was by now suffering from the early stages of acute altitude sickness, stopped me. He reasoned that if one person slipped, none of us would have a chance of getting an ice axe hold on the rock-hard ice surface beneath us. The mountain had long had a reputation of taking down strings of climbers, all pulled off by a single climber who had slipped at this very point.

We explained as best we could to the Sorrocco Alpino and they agreed to press on to the summit un-roped. I distinctly remember enjoying the feeling that I was totally responsible for my own life. Just as quickly, that responsibility was thrust upon me. As we neared the crest, I traversed an icy stretch from right to left and made the potentially fatal mistake of catching my crampons on the instep of my trousers. I tripped and instantly began to slide down the mountain. I fell on my ice axe, but carried on slipping as the axe ground against the ice face, sending a sharp spray of icy particles into my face. What seemed like minutes passed before the axe finally dug in and arrested my fall. Gingerly, I got to my feet and climbed back up to the rest of the team, who fortunately hadn't witnessed my debacle.

We made it to the lip of the volcano and got our first glimpse of the murky sulphur-laden crater, from which sinister wisps of smoke emerged far, far below. Hedley was really suffering now with the altitude and could go no higher. He signalled to us to climb on without him to the top of the volcano ridge some 1,000 feet beyond.

My first real taste of adventure at 17,802 feet on the summit
ridge of Mount Popocatépetl, Mexico, 1966.

I pushed on with one other of the Mexicans and stood at the
summit looking out at the incredible views. I whooped with joy at
being at the top of my first big peak at more than 17,000 feet and
fumbled with my camera to try to take a picture of my climbing
partner, but he was crouched down. To my embarrassment, I realised
that he was on his knees praying, tears running down the side of his

face. He later told me that it was a very emotional moment for him to reach the summit of Popocatépetl, having lost numerous friends to it over the years. That a summit could inspire such devotion was not lost on me. If I had ever doubted my potential to climb big mountains, Popocatépetl dispelled them. I had fallen in love with high-level climbing and the big peaks were beckoning to me.

— • —

After three years as an army officer, my senior officers were trying to persuade me to change from my short-service commission to a full-time engagement with the regiment. They offered me three months as an instructor in the winter warfare school if I promised to sign on as a regular officer. I was sorely tempted but knew somehow that I should move on. I remember that the decisive moment came while I was in a nightclub in Berlin, where we were posted at the time doing border controls. It was two in the morning and the music was playing. There were blue movies showing on the wall, endless beers and suddenly it hit me: this is the same as in Panama, Mexico, San Salvador, Belize, you name it. If I were to draw a graph of my life in the army in terms of learning and experience, it was starting to tail off. I needed to get a broader experience of life.

I had also fallen in love with an English girl that I had met while on exercises in Cyprus. We had started a deep correspondence while I was based in Berlin, wherein our relationship had blossomed. I knew then that this was the girl that I would ultimately marry. But she had told me that she could never stand being restricted to a "life

As a 2nd Lt. on army battle training in Cyprus in 1967.

on the patch", being penned in on a campus of army officer quarters. It was the final push that I needed.

Shortly after I left the army, I remember writing to my company commander and thanking him for teaching me so well, and for looking after me. I tried to explain my position and that as a young man of 21, I needed to learn more about life – about life in inner cities, about young people, about old people – people with real-life dramas. I knew as much as I was ever likely to learn about Staffordshire soldiers.

The commander wrote back to me to say that the army was a strange dichotomy in a way. For one, it gave you a huge amount of responsibility. As a young platoon commander, you would be trusted to go out in the foothills or the jungle with live ammunition and expected to deal, on your own, with whatever life threw at you. When war came, you had ultimate responsibility for the lives of your soldiers. And yet, in other ways, life was extraordinarily regimented and prescribed. Your clothes, your food, your equipment, the culture – these choices were all made for you.

I decided it was time I made some of my own. I joined the police as a constable and it would prove to be a very different life. When you were sent out on foot in those days, alone on your beat, apart from meal breaks, you were not expected to return to the police station – and, far from awaiting orders, it was frowned on if you telephoned for advice. You had to deal with anything that the day threw at you, from an injured horse that needed to be shot, to a lost child, or a drunken prostitute "importuning for immoral earnings". I had asked for broader life experience – and I got it.

THREE

Get Some Sea Room

By 1975, I was a 30-year-old police inspector with a team of my own operating out of Kentish Town Police Station. I had two good sergeants on my relief whom I was fortunate enough to also count as friends. Dave Morgan was a former Royal Navy man, while Keith Bateman was an ex-merchant Navy and "second mate" navigator and seaman. When we were on night duty in the police canteen and the weather was wild outside, they used to say to each other, "Remember being at sea on nights like this?"

Their eyes would glaze over as if in a trance, as if in that moment they were feeling the spray on their cheeks, the smell of sea salt in their nostrils. On one of these occasions, I said to them, "Look, you guys are always on about the sea, why don't we charter a boat and sail across the Atlantic!" They looked at each other, trying to work out if I was serious or not.

"You can't just do that," said Dave. "We'd need to start small – like going across the Channel."

I thought that sounded like an excellent idea. We hatched a plan in that moment and between the three of us found a 27-foot sloop,

Chayka of Ardour, recruited another sergeant, Dave Abbot, who raced 505 sailing dinghies for the British Police team, to be skipper; and I volunteered my cousin Richard to join us as a crewman. We would set off from Hamble to Cherbourg early one morning in September.

— • —

As the most inexperienced sailor on board, I was given the job of deck hand, as well as chief cook and bottle washer. Several hours into the crossing, I was just getting settled into my somewhat dubious duties in the cabin, when the boat bumped into the Isle of Wight – and I mean *bumped*, as in beached the sloop on a sand bar. Even to my tender talents, this didn't seem to bode well for our sailing captain's experience.

It was several hours before we could float the sloop off the sand – during which time we were visited by the coast guard, who regarded our story of having deliberately beached the boat to check the hull, as being a bit thin. Nevertheless, after some persuasion, they left us to our own devices, and some hours after that, we made it safely into harbour at Cherbourg. The voyage across the Channel had been cold, wet and boring and I'd spent much of it gazing endlessly into grey skies while the sloop made seemingly no progress for hours. I might have appreciated it more had I known what was in store for us on the journey back.

We whiled away the afternoon in Cherbourg port drinking beers with the crew of the *British Steel* – a large boat that had moored alongside us. As dusk drew in, we listened to the BBC weather forecast for the next day. It sounded reasonable, though our companions, who had been listening to the French forecast, were inclined to think otherwise. They told us the weather was likely to be considerably more serious and recommended taking the first tide at dawn.

In our ignorance, we had decided to trust the English forecast and hang on until 11 o'clock so that we could hit the duty-free shop when it opened, and stock up on whisky. Needless to say, when we awoke the next morning, the *British Steel* was long gone.

— • —

We set off from Cherbourg around midday, making our way gently through the harbour and eventually out into open sea harbour. We had been heading into a lively breeze for a couple of hours, when the skipper set up a transistor radio to listen into the weather forecast. I was perched further along the guardrails but remember hearing something along the lines of "… force eight or nine imminent…"

Everyone's faces dropped. I asked where this force eight would be, to which the reply was "right where we're heading". We deliberated over what to do, but we knew that with an onshore breeze, we would never make it back to Cherbourg before the storm hit. The only thing to do was to battle it out at sea.

It felt like no time at all before we were among waves that were fast building to mountainous proportions. I found it extraordinary how our little boat could clip down the slope of the wave, right down to the deepest trough, then miraculously ascend the near-vertical side of the waves coming towards us, and then helter-skelter down it again. Far from the drab grey boredom of the outward crossing, here we were right in the thick of it: this was exhilarating!

As the ordeal worsened, Keith's skills as a navigator were called upon. When we reached the peak of a wave, he would take a sextant reading on a radio beacon and then clamber below to plot our course. Doing just this, he somehow managed to get us as far as the Needles Lighthouse, just off the coast of the Isle of Wight.

At this point, the wind became cyclonic. The sails were flapping like crazy and it seemed impossible to set a straight course. We started veering towards the red zone of the lighthouse… towards the rocks.

"We need to get some sea room," yelled Keith – which meant getting out to sea, and that meant somehow turning the sloop to face back to France. We wrestled to get it round, until finally it broke free and shot out to sea with the huge wind and waves behind us.

By now, we were desperate to drop the mainsail, which had already swung round and cracked Dave Morgan on the head, leaving him with a nasty open wound. But every time we got an armful of the sail, the ship itself would wrench it free, threatening to throw us overboard. Eventually, we lashed it down, but now the foresail was far bigger than we needed and was taking us swiftly out to sea. We could have done with a storm jib, but the sheets had become knotted onto the guardrails and none of us had the strength, nor the courage, to go forward and untie them while the sloop thrust and heaved like a bucking bronco.

The skipper suddenly appeared from below deck with eyes like saucers.

"We have to get some help!" he yelled. He looked frightened as he came up on deck, lunging for the guardrails as he was caught off balance. He fired off a distress rocket, and to our surprise, it was answered almost immediately from land, a second long red, flare tail visible against the night sky. Unbeknown to us, the HMS Coastguard had been watching our progress and had us in their sights. Their response meant that the Royal National Lifeboat Institute boat at Yarmouth would be launched to come to our rescue.

— • —

Keith held the sloop on a straight course out to sea. His face spoke of deep concentration, but his eyes concealed a glint of excitement. He had navigated tankers all over the world, but had never experienced anything quite like this before in such a small boat. Dave Morgan had gone below to rest his split head, while the skipper, who I had a feeling was suffering from shock, had gone with him.

Perhaps the ordeal was easier for me than anyone else. This was, after all, my first outing in anything other than a sailing dinghy and I just assumed that this was how things went in a 27- foot sailing boat. I trusted the sloop to survive the storm and had nothing but confidence in Keith, who, by that point, had virtually taken over as skipper. This had not been an easy decision for him, he later explained to me. As far as he was concerned, the tradition at sea was that the skipper called the shots, and you didn't question his decisions or capability. But he could see when we made our way over to Cherbourg that perhaps Dave Abbot wasn't as experienced with large sea-going yachts as we'd first imagined. When the moment had called for it, though, he felt he had had no choice but to step up.

Sometime around midnight, Keith asked Richard and myself to man the helm while he went below for some rest. Richard had remained stalwart throughout the whole adventure and while he tried to hold a steady course, so that we would not end up sideways and risk rolling over on the huge waves behind us, I sat by the compass with a torch and relayed the readings to him. After a while, we started to see a consistent light behind us and realised that we were being followed by another boat. Relieved, we fired a distress flare to acknowledge that we'd spotted them.

But the sea that day wasn't sparing the lifeboat either. At some point, it had been so crushed by the oncoming waves that its radar was knocked out. Without a way to locate us, they were forced to call on the help of a Royal Navy vessel in the vicinity to help them get a fix on our position. The lifeboat crew had set off around midnight, saying goodbye to their loved ones – who later told us that they never expected to see their husbands alive again.

Gradually, the lifeboat gained ground on us, its lights getting brighter until, in the early hours of the morning, it came alongside our boat on the starboard side. The coxswain shouted across through a loudhailer that it was going to be impossible for them to take us in tow in these conditions or get a breeches buoy over to transfer us safely across. Would we jump?

Having heard the voices, our skipper came up on deck. I told him what the coxswain had asked and he shouted back an affirmative, "Yes!" The coxswain explained that he would do his best to get both

27

boats up on the same wave and that, one by one, we should jump for our lives. They would catch us and drag us on to the lifeboat.

That was the moment that our skipper handed over control of the boat to me.

"Take the helm, John, and whatever you do, keep going in a straight line."

There was no shortage of irony in this, given that I was by far the least experienced member of our meagre crew, but I took it willingly. For all the severity of the situation, I found myself enthralled by it. The worse it got, the more I felt I was coming into my own.

"I've got this covered," I told him, accepting the wheel.

I managed to keep the boat parallel as the lifeboat came up against us, the waves forcing it to crash into the side of the craft. The skipper was the first to jump. I assumed that he'd made it as the lifeboat drove away, getting ready for the second run-in.

The skipper was followed by the rest of the crew in succession, each hauled on board by lifeboat crew in their brightly coloured oilskins. Richard jumped wide, but his lifeline (an eight-foot safety rope), got caught in our rigging and he was left dangling from the ropes on the side of the lifeboat. I desperately tried to hold the boat's course, knowing that even the slightest change in direction would have crushed him between the two hulls. It felt like an eternity – though was likely no more than a few seconds – before one of the crewmen leant over with a knife and cut Richard free, hauling him on to the boat.

As the lifeboat pulled away one final time, the madness of the situation began to dawn on me. I remember laughing into the wind;

the devil in me rather fancied sailing off alone – though the thought did not last long. The lifeboat was coming in. I held our course, the gap gradually narrowed, six feet, four feet, and then, at the last minute, I scrambled onto the guardrails and jumped into the white of the spotlights and spray, trying to gain as much height as I could. I remember clinging onto the guardrails as the lifeboat crew picked me up and threw me onto the floor of the boat. I staggered to my feet and lurched across the swaying deck to the cabin. We had abandoned ship.

The lifeboat crew looked very serious. Just as I thought our troubles were over, theirs were just beginning. The coxswain had to find a way of turning the lifeboat 180 degrees to take us back to Yarmouth, and he had to do it at speed, lest we be caught sideways between waves and bowled over. How he did it that night, in such exacting conditions, I will never know.

It was strange, eerie almost, as we finally made our way into the quiet shelter of the harbour at Yarmouth – the adrenalin and drama of the previous 12 hours finally starting to ebb. I was filled with emotion as I stood there shaking hands with the men who had saved our lives.

— • —

Years later, I was at home when the telephone rang. It was a researcher from the TV programme *This is Your Life*.

"Is that John Peck?" I told her it was and she asked if I would be free to appear on the show.

"What, for me?" I asked.

"No, not you, Dave Kennett. He's retiring as coxswain from the Yarmouth lifeboat service and you're his most famous rescue."

I thought my crew would never stop laughing when I told them that I had thought I was the star of the show. I readily agreed to surprise Dave on the night. Through his unwavering steadiness and humility during our rescue, he had become a slightly mythical figure to me over the years, and I was grateful for the occasion to celebrate him.

The Yarmouth lifeboat going alongside the foundering sloop Chayka of Ardour, 14th September 1975.

Commemorative sketch of our rescue from the Channel in 1975 – one of the five most famous RNLI rescues of the 20th century. Credit: Mobil Oil Shipping Co Ltd.

Mobil Oil subsequently drew up commemorative etchings of the five most famous rescues of the 20th century, and we featured as one of those pictures. I still keep a copy as a reminder of the feeling that I had that day as I held the wheel in those last moments before the rescue. It was perhaps my first indication that I could exist there, on the dark side of what I had previously thought was impossible, and it was a feeling I would come to regard rather like an old friend in the years to come.

Dave Abbott, our skipper, had taken a while to come back to work after our ordeal, and probably suffered from what would now be called post-traumatic stress. But in fairness to him, his sailing experience had probably told him how serious the situation was at the time, whereas I had been blessed with a naive innocence that can sometimes be an advantage when conditions are extreme.

The realisation that you can handle those extremes can, on the one hand, create hedonistic, even narcissistic, tendencies – like someone who has experienced their first heroin hit and is desperate for more. But on the other, when you emerge from such challenges, you certainly feel, in a quiet way, that everything is possible. The two can be a potent combination.

When, in the early Noughties, I first started to consider the possibility of rowing across the Atlantic, people would say to me: "Do you realise your little boat will have 30-foot waves coming after it for most of the time you're out there?"

I remember thinking that I'd faced Force 10 gales and 30-foot waves then, and it hadn't felt so bad. Though quite by accident, my boundaries had been pushed wider than perhaps most people. I had faced down my fear then, so the thought of extending it a bit further was logical, even reasonable. Wasn't it?

FOUR
So Near, So Far

I was sitting in my office at the police station when I came across an article about "one of Britain's best-kept secrets", the Three Peaks Yacht Race. Inspired by the legendary climber and sailor Bill Tillman who'd lived in Barmouth, the race takes in 389 miles up the west side of the UK and includes a run of some 70-odd miles with 11,000 feet of climbing and sailing in "some of the most exciting waters the country has to offer", the article said.

The first run had only been a few years ago, in 1977, by a group of local runners and sailors. They set sail from Barmouth on the Welsh coast to Fort William in Scotland, stopping along the way to take in the three highest peaks in the British Isles. This meant sailing in to Caernarvon, running 23.5 miles from the harbour to the top of Mount Snowdon and back; then on to Ravenglass in Cumbria, where you had to run 35 miles to the summit of Scafell Pike; and then sail on round to Fort William and the final 15-mile leg to the top of Ben Nevis.

The whole race took three or four days and mixed 'yachties' (yachtsmen who tend to take sailing, and themselves, very seriously), 'fell runners' (an irreverent lot with the character and stamina of mountain goats) and 'roadies' (often serious-minded, solitary types who ran marathons and were obsessed with personal bests). I couldn't put myself in any of those groups exactly, but I was gripped and I decided, there and then, to sign up a team for the following year.

— • —

A Metropolitan Police constable called John Stickland was the first person that I roped in. He was an exemplary officer, but I knew that he found it rather tedious when his work on the beat got in the way of his real passion – sailing. He was a Lt. Commander in the Royal Navy Reserves, a badge he wore with pride, and there was an air of the swashbuckler about him. Next had been Keith Bateman, the former-Navy seaman who had pulled us back from the brink of disaster in the Channel in 1975. He would navigate while John acted as skipper. A 26-year-old PC called Spike Milligan would accompany me on the first leg up to Snowdon, but I still needed to find a runner to join me on last two mountains. That's when I'd thought of Trog.

Trog Royle worked in the Public Order Training Section coaching the riot police. An ex-Royal Marine, he still served as an unarmed combat instructor in his spare time at the Marine Reserves in Lympstone and had trained the notorious "Special Boat Service". Legends about him were rife.

More often than not, his role training the riot police was to be "The Nutter". He'd have to pretend to hole himself up in a room, refusing to come out, and we would have to try to extricate him while he ranted abuse and wielded 4x2 chunks of wood at us. When he wasn't doing that, he was preparing Molotov cocktails. He would line up 10 at a time on the training ground and hurl them at us as we advanced towards him in our fireproof overalls, sweaty palms gripping our riot shields. Occasionally, he would try to liven things up by setting fire to himself and rushing towards us – whereby we would have to try to get him to the ground and spray him with a fire extinguisher. Trog generally came out unscathed, but it was hard to tell because his face was so craggy. He used to blame it on the ugly pills he was taking.

His sense of humour was as legendary as his antics. We had once been running together in a mountain marathon race when he suddenly declared, "I must stop for a crap, sir!" (he always called me sir, despite me persistently asking him to call me John). With that, he promptly jumped into a dip in a peat bog, lowered his back and rucksack against the peat wall, and dropped his shorts. Just at that moment, another runner appeared behind us. He stopped his tracks and quite out of the blue, said to Trog, "Don't I know you? Aren't you a wrestler or something?"

"I don't know," Trog yelled out of the mist, "but I am wrestling with this turd right now!"

All this, as well as the fact that he was an ex-bootneck who loved messing about on boats, made Trog an obvious choice for the Three Peaks Race. He also seemed to be able to endure pain indefinitely. Given the task ahead, this struck me as quite an asset.

— • —

The first leg from Caernarvon went relatively smoothly. I found the climb up and down Snowdon hard – much harder than I had expected – and as I reached Llanberis at the base of the mountain with eight miles to go to Caernarvon, my strength was sapped. The sun was scorching and I was starting to walk up the hills, while Spike built up a lead in front of me. I had warned our support team that I would need a kick in the pants at this point and, fortunately, they were there in the Land Rover to hound us on: "Come on, don't let Spike beat you. Catch him up!" I shuffled into a slow run for a while and then dropped back until they were next in sight.

Finally, with just three miles to go, I suddenly felt the weight of responsibility I had on me to see our team through: we had planned to do this leg in four and half hours, and well over four hours had now passed. We would have to really push it if we were going to stick to the plan. I felt the hair stand up on the back of my neck and that strange, tingling feeling as a deeper inspiration started to trickle through my body. I caught up to Spike, who by now had sunk into despair, his body functioning merely mechanically, and urged him on into the outskirts of Caernarfon.

At last, we reached the town and, as we rounded a corner, there was the familiar mast of our boat and a crowd of spectators. The adrenalin surged and we ran for the boat – we'd made it in four hours, 33 minutes.

We slipped out of the port into the open sea for the next leg of the voyage to Ravenglass – only to spend much of the next two days becalmed. Luckily, anticipating that this might happen, before we had left Caernarvon, our support crew had managed to fix up some homemade wooden rowlocks on the deck and "borrowed" two 18-foot-long whaler rowing oars. We now unleashed these and set about trying to row the boat against the current that seemed determined to take us backwards.

We rowed for hours. It was monotonous and gruelling work, but we were rewarded when we saw that we were inching our way past one of our competitors. To celebrate, Trog put on an old skirt and hat that he had found in the cabin and, after bolstering himself up in the appropriate places, cavorted about the deck blowing kisses to our rivals.

— • —

We arrived at the mouth of Ravenglass estuary at five o'clock in the morning – one hour too late to get the boat into the shallows and drop Trog and me off on dry land. We had chosen a Class Three ocean racer with a big keel because it was fast out at sea, but now we needed to get into harbour and that big keel was stopping us. Since five o'clock we'd been anchored offshore, pacing about the boat waiting – waiting for our chance to get in and start the 35-mile run up to the peak of Scafell Pike and back. We had never run that distance before, let alone run it carrying rucksacks with 10lb of survival gear and, having already psyched ourselves up for the challenge at dawn, we were bitterly disappointed not to have been able to start on time.

Finally, it was time to hit land again and it was raining hard, the boat was starting to pitch about. Trog and I went down below and changed out of our wet oilskins into flimsy running gear. We looked out of the hatch as the rain was falling steadily and a breeze was starting to whistle through the rigging above the deck. It seemed so dull and unwelcoming outside the warmth of the cabin. Trog shut the hatch and we both looked at each other as if to say, "What the hell are we doing this for?"

The engine started on the boat and we knew it was now only minutes before we had to get out there. We shouldered our rucksacks and made our way up on deck as the anchor chain went in. A short trip ashore in the rubber boat and then Trog and I were running through the shallows towards the marshal who would clock us in for the next stage of the race.

The run to the base of Scafell will stay in my mind forever. Having been away at sea for a few days, we were suddenly aware of the sounds and smells of the countryside. The gentle fragrance of honeysuckle and rhododendrons and the soft light of the evening soothed us after the barren harshness of the sea. Trog pointed to some lambs and said gently, "Aren't they sweet?" I wasn't sure if he was joking – it seemed so incongruous to see this rough, tough Marine moved by a lamb. Maybe he was talking about how they'd taste.

We reached Wasdale Head after some 16 miles and set off up the mountain proper. It was pouring with rain now and getting dark. Trog led the pace up to the ridge of Scafell, stopping only once to greet a couple of our support crew who had bravely faced the elements to bring us a hot drink half way up the hill (how much we appreciated their fortitude!). By the time we reached the summit, we were drenched to the skin. We had been so desperate to reach it before nightfall that we hadn't stopped to put on more clothes, and now we were surrounded by a cold mist.

We took off along a line of cairns down the ridge. We had descended about 600 feet when I shouted to Trog to stop. Despite the obvious line of the path, we seemed to be heading off our bearing. As we huddled round the map, the wind picked up and the heavens opened again. We couldn't afford to waste time getting lost – in an effort to keep our kit to a minimum, to reduce weight, we were poorly equipped to survive a night on the mountain.

We climbed back up to the summit, took a fresh bearing and then carefully picked our way down the ridge until we were sure of the way. So relieved to find ourselves back on the right route, we bounded down and away from that dark hell at alarming speed. Just over four hours had elapsed since we left the boat in Ravenglass and we knew that the remaining 15 miles or so could easily be done within the six and half hour cut off target that we had set ourselves.

After more hot, sweet coffee with our support crew at the base of Scafell, we pushed on along the road skirting Lake Wastwater and back to the coast. I turned and shouted through the wind at the mountain – taunting it for having failed to outwit us – but perhaps I shouldn't have done that. Fate has a strange way of exacting its vengeance, as we were about to find out.

— • —

We passed another group of runners who had set out two hours before us and felt pleased with ourselves. We picked up the pace. We were making good time and knew that we couldn't rejoin the boat yet, which would be coming in on the early morning tide, so we made for where our support crew was camping in Ravenglass, overjoyed to find that they had hot showers and even a hot breakfast ready for us when we arrived.

Shortly before six o'clock and feeling restored, we picked up our rucksacks and made our way to the water's edge to wait for the boat to pick us up. Half past six came and still they hadn't appeared. We paced up and down, desperately searching the horizon, but could see no sign of them approaching. What the hell had happened to them? Maybe they had just overslept? Eventually it dawned on us that something must have gone wrong. One of the lads went off to phone the coast guard, returning 10 minutes later, grim-faced.

"We've blown it," he said.

Slowly the story emerged. After dropping us ashore the previous evening, Spike, John and Keith had promptly spun the yacht around and headed back out into the bay where they found a sheltered spot to drop anchor. But just as the storm had raged on the mountain, the wind had blown into a fierce gale out at sea, making it unsafe to stay where they were. They'd decided to move off and ride out the storm overnight at sea.

In order to be able to take up the anchor, you have to motor the vessel up into the wind until it's almost directly above the anchor itself and then heave it up. But when John started the motor, he found that the boat wouldn't move forward. Keith tried to heave in the anchor rope himself, but to no avail. He put the rope onto a winch and tried to winch it in by hand, and then again using his feet to push the winch handle, but still nothing. The force of the wind by now was pushing the boat in the other direction, making it impossible for them to make any headway. They were going to have to abandon their anchor, leave it attached to a float and hope to pick it up later once the storm abated.

All night out at sea the three of them wrestled with the boat, with no respite. When daylight finally came, John had again tried the engine, but found that it still wouldn't draw them forward. Keith volunteered to dive down under the boat with a mask on to inspect the propeller. He said the water had been so cold that it took his breath away. When, after three dives, he finally clambered back on board, gibbering, it was with devastating news. The propeller must have become unscrewed, because it was now missing altogether.

John tried to decide what to do. The wind had finally dropped, the tide was coming in and the boat was drifting into the lee shore. But without their anchor or the engine functioning, there was no way that he could get the boat into Ravenglass – or indeed to any other port, to pick up the runners. With a sick feeling in his stomach, he was forced to summon help from the coast guard, who managed to send out a lifeboat from Workington, 20 miles up the coast, to tow them into port. The race was over.

— • —

The field was bathed in that early morning sunlight that trickles lazily through the branches, falling like searchlights on the mist-covered grass below. There was no breeze and no sound, but for the buzzing of insects going about their business. I sat alone on the edge of the field looking down across the valley towards the sea, and thought how different it was to the optimism of the previous evening when we had entered Ravenglass estuary.

I heard a shepherd's whistle and then saw a flash of black and white moving towards the sheep below, the dog worrying them all until they grudgingly moved into another field. I thought how the calm, tough acceptance of most country folk in this part of the world must be moulded by a gradual acceptance of the inevitability of the elements: the defeats when they seem to be against you and the unexpected rewards when they're with you.

I thought of my father, whose own fatalistic approach to life had always inspired me, and I remembered an occasion when I had gone to him in tears as a boy after one failure or another.

"Don't worry John, it's all for the best," he said. "After all, you'll never know what unhappy circumstances you would have met if you had succeeded."

I smiled at the thought of it now and wondered if he might be right his time.

I looked around and saw Trog hanging up his wet clothes on the wooden fence behind me and called him over. Neither of looked at each other, but sat watching the sheep dog.

"Sorry guv, I had to go off on my own for a while there. I cried my bloody eyes out," he said.

I told him we'd come back next year and win, but he didn't look convinced.

We drove to Workington to see the lifeboat towing our yacht into the harbour. It was a sad sight. Local newspaper and TV reporters clustered about the harbour walls like vultures. Both John and Keith were trying to put on a brave face but looked pretty shattered. The whole scene seemed macabre. Photographers scrabbling about, cameras clicking.

I looked at John and he shrugged his shoulders.

"Sorry John," he said, " the wheel fell off the bike."

— • —

With the crew ashore, we feverishly arranged to get hold of another propeller. We had chartered the boat for a drop off in Scotland, so we had to get it there one way or another. The nearest propeller available was in Essex and arrangements were made to get it brought up to Workington by courier for nine o'clock the next morning. We found a diver prepared to fit it, and with that, the crippled yacht was moved into the inner harbour for the night.

The following day Trog and Spike had decided to go on by land to Fort William to climb the last hill. Trog said he couldn't face the embarrassment of arriving by boat. So, it was left to John, Keith and I to take the boat and its new propeller up to Scotland. It seemed empty somehow, without Trog and Spike – as if part of the family was missing. The wind came up almost immediately after we left. We were now to see the power of the beautiful craft in which we sailed and, sadly, to realise how well we could have fared against the other craft in the race had we got to this point in one piece.

Our arrival at Fort William at half past nine on Saturday morning passed almost unnoticed; most of the competitors having already left for home. This was in stark contrast to the carnival atmosphere of our departure, when the fleet of 35 sailing craft had set out from Barmouth past harbour walls covered with spectators.

We tidied up the boat and Keith and I decided that we would climb the last of the mountains now that we were here. In some ways it was a pleasant break to be able to move at a leisurely pace. The day was warm and visibility crystal clear. Ben Nevis, which had apparently been shrouded in mist for the past three days, offered up to us views for miles around. Keith and I shook hands on having reached the summit and sat for while looking down the mountainside to the tranquil coastline beyond.

After days of storms, the air was now so calm that had we dropped a feather, it would had floated gently all the way to the bottom.

FIVE

Rewarded At Ravenglass

After our first attempt at the Three Peaks Yacht Race had been cruelly cut short, I had resolved on that hill above Ravenglass that if I never went on another adventure again, I would finish this race… and finish it well.

Our catamaran *Triple Fantasy* with added whaler oars for when the wind dropped.

I knew Keith and John wanted to have another go and that Trog would come round – despite protesting that he was getting too old and that the previous year was supposed to have been his "last big effort". In the end, neither John nor Spike could make it. That meant that we needed a new skipper and, for what I had in mind, we needed someone with a strong track record of racing big boats. Another detective inspector from the Met Police, Alex Ross, turned out to be our man.

For this year's race, I had managed to charter a brightly-coloured trimaran named *Triple Fantasy*. This was a yacht with three hulls – with the two outer ones resembling long canoes, while the central section had a slim cabin that you could just about squeeze two people into – or three at pinch. After being held up for so long waiting for a full tide to get us into Ravenglass the previous year, I wanted something with a shallow draught that might give us an advantage over some of the other boats with bigger keels – and *Triple Fantasy* was just the ticket.

We stripped absolutely everything off the boat that didn't make it go fast, including the small stove. We resolved to live off sandwiches provided by our land support crew and whatever else they could rustle up when we were onshore. This was a racing boat and we really were going to race it this time.

When Alex first came aboard, I told him how serious we were about the race this year and he said he was prepared to push the boat to its limits for us if that's what we wanted. But we had to understand, he said, that given the trimaran's large sail area, when we were moving fast and the boat was leaning over, one hull would come out of the water and start lifting into the air. When it got high enough out of the water, the opposite hull would start to go underwater. If it went deep enough under, it could dig in and trip the whole boat up on its nose. If it flipped us over, we were finished, because the only thing that could right us would be a crane.

I discussed it with the crew, and we all agreed that we were prepared to take the risk if it meant getting on the podium.

— • —

Trog Royle and I at Caernarvon preparing to run the
first leg to the top of Snowden and back.

With Spike out, Trog would accompany me on all the runs this year. As with the previous year, the first run up to Snowdon and back went well and we were soon away from Caernarvon and, thanks to our shallow draught, dancing through the Menai Straits – gaining ground on some of the other boats that had managed to get away before us.

Trog and I were lying in our small bunks in the hull recuperating, when the wind whipped up suddenly and the boat lurched forward like an eager dog on a leash. We could feel the whole boat start to hum and hear Alex whooping with excitement. Gradually, one hull started to lift a little. At first, we would hear it slapping on the water, and then there would be silence except for the wind on the sails, as the hull became airborne. Trog and I looked at each other at this point with nervous excitement, then one of us reached for where the axe was fitted – knowing that if the boat flipped upside down, our only means of escape would be to hack our way out.

— • —

We sneaked into Ravenglass harbour in the early hours of the morning without hiccup. We were several hours ahead of our time the previous year. Spurred on by this, Trog and I set off at a good pace, making it to the foot of the mountain at Wasdale Head ahead of schedule – and then foolishly tried something new. I had got hold of some thick chocolate drinks before we'd left and we now swigged these down assuming they would give us strength for the mountain. Wrong move. In the heat of the day, the blood ran down to our stomachs, eager to digest the rich sugary drink and, before we knew it, we were hyperglycaemic. On, on, up, up we struggled, feeling depressed and weak as babies.

It wasn't until we got to the summit of Scafell Pike that we started to regain our energy. The only thing that had kept us going was our marvellous support crew – many of the old faces were back again for this second attempt – who would cheer us on and, every so often, pour cold water over us to liven us up. As we came off the mountain and hit the road from Wasdale back to the harbour, it was often only a glimpse of their Land Rover turning a corner ahead that would force us out of our painful reverie and break into a run again.

I have never been so glad to climb into a boat as when we finally arrived in Ravenglass after those nightmarish 35 miles. But instead of jumping for joy that, this time, our boat was here ready to take us on to the next stage of the race, I remonstrated myself for losing time on the run: why had I brought those bloody chocolate drinks? I swore I wouldn't go trying anything new again, if what I'd already been doing was working just fine.

Our sailing crew were good enough to laugh it off. They knew that we had taken far too long on that leg of the race, but could see that we felt terrible and said nothing, ushering us to our bunks to get some rest while they made way.

After about a half hour of sailing, I remember Alex coming down into the cabin to get a bag of sails from the forward locker. Having dragged the sail bag out, he dumped it on a locker and then turned back into the cabin. Through eyes half asleep, I saw him take off his fleece jacket and lay it over Trog's sleeping body before climbing out on deck. Trog slept on, blissfully unaware of this simple act of kindness, but in my weary state, it was enough to move me to tears. This was a special team, I thought.

— • —

One thing that we had noticed on our previous attempt was that it wasn't too much wind that was the biggest hazard, but too *little*. Being becalmed is misery to a sailor. The more experienced skippers know just where to find a bit of wind, even if it's just a little, but, one time or another, everyone becomes becalmed and the boat sits listlessly, sails flapping gently. Having thought long and hard about how we would deal with this, we resolved to employ the same strategy as the previous year, when we had managed to get ourselves out of the doldrums by commandeering a pair of old whaler oars at Caernarvon. This time, we'd stowed a pair on board from the start and had even practised rowing ourselves out of trouble, so that as soon as we were becalmed, we whipped them out and heaved to.

As the wind died at the Mull of Kintyre, we rowed past the the Royal Marine team in their First Class sailing boat for the the third or fourth time, feeling unstoppable. They later told us that they dreaded seeing our oars come out.

We arrived at Fort William in second position, with the Royal Marines close behind us. We knew their runners well and knew that they were strong. We'd met them in the bar before the start of the race and they never seemed to stand still, just kept jigging up and down.

Trog and I donned our running gear and prepared ourselves for the 15 hard miles up to Ben Nevis. We agreed that we were going for it "shit or bust". If one of us got injured, the other would carry them. Whatever it took, nothing would stop us finishing this race. We knew that we might be slower than the Marines on the climb, so our plan was to get to the summit as quickly as we could and then, on the descent, instead of following the wide zig-zag track, we would cut all the corners and just plunge straight down the mountainside over the rough ground to make up time.

We must have reached the top just seconds before the Marines, because no sooner had we noticed that they were behind us, they broke away to begin the descent. Annoyed at having been overtaken and unsure who else might be close on the climb up, we put our direct-descent plan into action. I was ahead of Trog when I suddenly heard a yelp and then a thud. He had tripped and was rolling down the hill. I made my way over to where he'd finally stopped; I could see he'd badly injured his ankle. I offered him my hand and suggested that I carry his rucksack for him.

He looked defiantly at me.

"Nobody carries my rucksack, sir!" he said, staggering to his feet. He started hobbling as fast as he could, leaving me to fall in behind.

Sometimes with ankle injuries you can be lucky and run through them until the pain eases off, but I don't think this was happening in Trog's case. It was just sheer bloody mindedness that got him down that mountain until, once back on dirt tracks, he was able to turn his hobbling into a slow, limping run and keep plugging away at the miles.

— • —

The finishing posts appeared in the distance, red and white tape across them. We hadn't caught the Marines, but we were in third position and that was good enough for us. With less than a hundred metres to go, the reality that we would make it washed over us both like a wave. We wrapped our arms around each other through the tape, landing in a heap on the floor, much to the amusement of our chums from the Marines who had waited to see us in.

Chuffed to bits with our podium finish in Fort William.

It was an unforgettable moment: a dream that had magically come true after more than two years of hard work and disappointment. Trog and I felt like a couple of amateurs who had somehow made it to the FA Cup Final. And I suppose that was about right: I wasn't a marathon runner or a fell runner, really, and while I had done plenty of both of those things, I was never likely to have been among the winners. Nor was I a sailor. This was only my third trip as a crew member on a yacht. But if I knew what I wasn't, then I also knew what I was. I was an adventurer – and being an adventurer means being able to turn your hand to anything that will enable you to make that adventure actually happen. All else is dreaming.

SIX

The Matterhorn Doesn't Give Itself To Everyone

Climbing trips up to Wales and Scotland proved to be a refreshing interlude from the rigours of inner-city police life in London, and I longed for these chances to get out into the hills to re-energise before getting back into the fray. I had started fell running in my late 20s and so would enter mountain marathon races each year with friends, which were inevitably held in wild rocky territory in the Lake District, North Wales or the Highlands. The experience of running down mountains when you are young and fit is nothing short of exquisite. At times, it would feel like flying, as my legs just seemed to skim the surface of the mountain as we floated down it at speed in a kind of meditative dream.

These were some of the happiest and most exhilarating moments of my life, even if they brought with them their share of pain, as we toiled our way up and down the rugged mountain in the mist and cold searching for the flags that marked secluded checkpoints. Halfway through the event, we would sleep out in makeshift campsites on the side of the mountain, our tents dotted among those of the hundreds of other competitors, steam rising from our small gas stoves, as warm as the banter and camaraderie that we shared.

As someone with something of an extrovert personality, the company of a fellow adventurer is a vital part of the experience and adds much to the fun of these events. When, at times, your energy and enthusiasm flags, I have always found that the sense of humour of your companion is more valuable than any other piece of vital equipment in keeping you going.

Climbing on Shepherd's Crag in the Lake District with some of the BOLAC club.

By the mid-1970s, I was meeting more and more people who wanted to experience the mountains but didn't quite have the confidence to do it by themselves. I pulled some climbing friends together and decided to start a climbing club. We called the club BOLAC, which I think was meant to stand for Beer And Lots Of Climbing, but we didn't quite manage to get the letters in the right order before we had the T-shirts made. The group grew as friends of friends were invited to join, and in its heyday the club had more than 20 active members.

Chief protagonist among these was one of the warmest characters that I've ever met, Alan Caudell. He was a true London "geezer" with a ginger beard, a Michael Caine accent and an insatiable appetite for beer, so much so that it was hard to fathom how he remained as slim as a whippet and moved so fast up a mountain – but he did. Alan had set up his own property company and at the height of his success had, on a whim, bought a remote farmhouse just beneath the mountain, Skiddaw. Nestled in the valley, there wasn't another house in sight. It was called Derwent Folds. One of the chief reasons that he had bought it was so that his climbing chums could meet there. Come February each year, snow descended on the Lake District and this became our target for a few days each winter.

Wild days of blizzards around the mountains and spectacular views of frozen sunlit landscapes at dawn were part of the joy of those days – topped only by the copious pints of local beer that we would see off in Keswick after we descended from the mountain, often in the dark, to our favourite pub – The Dog and Gun.

As the evening wore on, the singing would begin, and sometimes I would bring along a guitar to liven it up. Our aim, inevitably, would be to build a human pyramid in the middle of the pub – much to the chagrin of the landlord who would always try to stop us, though, invariably it was too late. We graduated from here to what we called "bar diving". This involved one person crouching on the bar and leaping into the arms of his chums, who were meant to catch him. I say "meant to" because very often, after half a dozen pints, the increasingly complex catching strategies that we employed got muddled.

The BOLAC crew on one of climbing trips in the Lakes.

Variations started to emerge such as "The Quick Draw Method". This involved the catchers standing in two rows on either side of the diver's flight path with their hands at their sides. Then, when the jumper took off, if they were quick enough, they could grasp the wrists of the person opposite them before the jumper landed. But, all too often, the beer and the raucous laughter would get the better of us, leaving the jumper to land on a crumpled pile of giggling catchers. These were happy times; unburdened by any cares that we might have had before arriving in the Lakes.

Winter in the Lakes provided no shortage of peaks for snow and ice climbing and I found that I could take on quite testing climbs without too much difficulty. I had decided to take a week-long course, and the pinnacle of our week away was a two-day expedition into the heart of the Cairngorms to a place where we could dig caves into the deep snowdrifts. Once inside, the caves were warm as toast and you could strip right down to a single layer and still feel cosy in there.

Enamoured by the mountains, and the ease with which I seemed to have become accustomed to climbing on the ice, and with the winter climbing course behind me, I felt ready for more. I was approaching 39 by this time and I knew that I would have to test myself in the Alps.

— • —

I had heard of a company called Mountain Ventures that led groups on a week's alpine training, followed by a climb of the Matterhorn. I pulled a group of BOLAC climbers together – including my cousin Richard and pal Alan, my oldest climbing partners – and we set off for the Alps. Arriving in Zermatt, Switzerland, we located our hostel and found it had a direct view of the Matterhorn. In fact, wherever you go in Zermatt, the Matterhorn dominates your thoughts, beckoning you towards it. It's not surprising that is one of the world's most iconic peaks.

For several days, we dedicated ourselves to learning the Alpine way, climbing peaks such as Rimpfischhorn and Alphubel. I felt strong and was probably at the peak of my fitness. Just as the team were ready to take on the Matterhorn itself, it was deemed "out of condition": covered in mist and far too much snow. It was so frustrating to wait at the bottom, ready to go, watching as the days ticked by – time running out before the team were due to fly home.

On the last night, I decided that I would stay on. Before I left the UK, I had promised to use the expedition to the Matterhorn to raise enough money in sponsorship to buy a radio hearing aid for a little girl called Danielle and was determined to hang on for as long as I could to get a shot at the summit.

Before the others left to go home, we had one final night of celebrations. Alan, having survived a week's climbing in the Alps, found himself dancing on an upturned barrel that night, only to fall off into a crowd of locals, and was forced to limp to the airport the next morning, grinning all the way. It was so sad to see my good friends go back. It felt very lonely and serious after they had left.

One of the guides who had been training us that week was called Roger Baxter Jones. Roger was a guy in his early 30s with a strong track record of Alpine and big peak ascents, and when he heard about my quest, he offered, for a reasonable fee, to help guide me to the summit.

We set off for the Hornli Hut, which sat at around 10,700 feet, and waited for the weather to clear. We were up at that hut for several days and, each day, I would run all the way down into Zermatt to get more food and walk up again to keep fit for the climb. On one of these occasions, I was stopped by Frau Biner, the owner of the Bahnhof Hotel, where we were staying and which to this day is the accommodation most British climbers choose to use when in Zermatt.

"Are you trying again?" she said, referring to the climb. I told her I was and she looked up at the mountain, bathed in snow and mist, and shook her head. "You are very courageous."

The Matterhorn from Zermatt in 1983.

Somewhat disconcerted by what Frau Biner had meant by this last remark, I mentioned it to Roger back at the hut. He laughed. "She doesn't speak very good English," he said. "I'm sure she just meant 'very persistent'!"

A few days later, I picked up a call from my wife. She told me that my boss at the police station was "going mad" that I wasn't back. He told her that if I didn't return quick, he would discipline me on charge of being absent from duty. I told Roger of my predicament. He promised that we would set off before dawn the next day and take the mountain on as a winter ascent.

"The risks of falling will be great," he said. "It's up to you if you are prepared to take those risks, but I can't guarantee our safe return."

With some conviction, I told him I wasn't returning without having climbed the mountain and at four o'clock the next morning, we set off into the darkness, with only the light of our head torches picking out the way ahead as we started up the slopes of the climb.

In the early stages, the trail is difficult to find and what trail there is is littered with loose scree and rubble. Despite this, we moved quickly and in what seemed like no time at all, we were ascending the Hornli Ridge – a sharp, knife-edge ridge that brings you round to face Zermatt. Here, Roger told me that it was possible in the icy conditions for one of us to slip down one side of the ridge. Roped together 15–20 feet from each other, he instructed me that if he were to fall down one side of the ridge, I was to throw myself down the other side to save him. Needless to say, this focused the mind somewhat.

We made our way up past the small Solvay Hut and onto the snow and ice climb beyond until we faced the crest of the summit.

This section was made easier by a series of fixed ropes. These were gymnasium-style truck ropes anchored to the rock in places, which you could pull on for security with one hand as you climbed up in your crampons, your ice axe in the other hand.

As dawn broke, we were near the shoulder of the mountain, the whole of which was bathed in a pink glow. The colours of the horizon looked quite beautiful and I wished that I had the camera equipment to reproduce them accurately.

The sun warmed us as we set off across the snow-laden shoulder that had kept us at bay for so long. The snow made a crisp crunch underfoot and we were easily able to cut footsteps up towards the summit. All around us the snow was unmarked. It had been more than two weeks since the last team had made it to the summit, so there was no sign of footprints.

After four hours of climbing, we reached the summit and climbed the frozen ridge to the highest point. We looked out over the opposite side from our approach, towards Italy, and were greeted with a view of tranquil countryside.

Roger said it was the fastest time in which he had ever reached the summit. Not bad considering that the mountain had been declared "out of condition" in the days leading up to it. I felt an amazing surge of emotion as we stood on top of this beautiful mountain, which had so nearly been denied to us. I remembered back to the time when I had climbed Popocatépetl and how a Mexican climbing with me had fallen to his knees in tears on reaching the summit. Now I understood why. Roger, too, was infected with the same emotion and embraced me at the top, shrieking in happiness at the top of his voice. We must

Ecstatic at having reached the top of the Matterhorn after so many days waiting.

have looked a crazy pair to those down below peering up at us through binoculars.

After savouring the solitude unique to such a spot, we started the long descent. Descents of mountains are notoriously dangerous and more people die descending mountains like the Matterhorn than on the way up. Once you have reached the summit it is easy to get euphoric and light-headed, and clumsy moves can very easily snatch you and your climbing partner to an early death.

The snow was melting in the morning sun and parts of the route were becoming treacherous. It was a great comfort to have someone such as Roger on the other end of the rope, for it was his strength and experience that got us down in one piece.

Once down at the Hornli Hut, Roger and I enjoyed two well-earned bottles of beer and packed away our climbing gear. I had hoped to get the Téléphérique cable car back down to the town, but when I got there, crowds of skiers were waiting. Having used up virtually all my cash, I was desperate to make it to the bank in Zermatt before it shut. I decided to run down the remaining 4,500 feet to town. I didn't stop once; my head was in the clouds and my heart in a place of utter glory.

Sometimes I talk to groups that I'm training about being "in the zone", when everything comes together. This was one of those moments and the memories of that climb will remain with me, like an elixir, for the rest of my life.

I arrived at the bank with five minutes to spare, feeling dazed and euphoric, my ears popping like crazy. The guy behind the counter looked at me in confusion as I stood there panting and bathed in

The late Roger Baxter Jones who led me to my first summit of the Matterhorn.

sweat, the pen slipping between my fingers. He kept asking in German, "What is the hurry?" I hadn't the heart to tell him where I had come from.

When I returned to the Bahnhof Hotel, Frau Biner, met me and warmly clasped me by the hand. She could tell by the look on my face that we had made it.

"Well done," she said. "You deserve the prize. The Matterhorn does not give itself up to everyone."

I understood what she meant.

The views at the summit of the Matterhorn had been stunning, so much so that I could see how people would chose to spend their lives as guides, living forever in the mountains.

Roger had been emotional as we approached the metal cross at the summit and I saw tears in his eyes. He told me that there were several mountains that he had climbed that were quite spiritual and this was one of them.

Looking back, the moment seemed so prescient; tragically, before the year was up, an avalanche on Mont Blanc would take Roger and, unfortunately, we would never have the opportunity to climb with each other again.

SEVEN
6529

S htuck, shtuck. Shtuck, shtuck. I fastened another screw into the ice, clipped on the carabiner, pulled the rope through and climbed on. Behind me, Lew climbed, collecting all of the ice screws as he went.

We had been moving fluidly like this for six hours. Somewhere below, the two Steves were doing the same. There had been nothing around us but blue skies – the only sound that of our gear clanking against the sheer ice face. But now, as we looked down along the valley, dark clouds were gathering quickly. It soon started snowing. Lew caught up to me: whether we turned back now or not, the storm would still hit us, he said, best to push on to the ridge above, where we hoped to be able to pitch the tent and ride it out.

Our target was a peak with no name. We were deep in the Garhwal Himalayas and our map identified it simply as "6529". It was one giant snow and ice face rising up 3,000 feet to a crest at its highest point. We'd been looking up at it every day for almost four weeks – ever since we'd been in the Jogin mountain range, seduced by the clean, crisp lines that separated it from other scruffier peaks.

We'd chosen to attempt a climb of the north face that would take us up to the mountain's north-west ridge. The most obvious line of approach was the ice face itself and then a steep mile-long ascent up a snow-covered ridge to the summit. Now, here we were, two thirds of the way up the ice face – the wind howling; trying to tear us from the rock.

As the storm came in, we fought our way up to a gully – a sort of half-pipe flanked by rocky outcrops – that led to an overhanging cliff that we had planned to pitch our tent under.. The gully had been funnelling a constant torrent of snow out and down the mountain all day, but as I got nearer and nearer, the rush of snow suddenly stopped, as if some giant, invisible arm was holding it back.

The north face of Peak 6529 in the Garhwal Himalayas in northern India.

I took the opportunity to move quickly through, hammering metal pegs into the exposed rock where I could; conscious that they would probably be little use to us if we fell. I hacked and hauled upwards, desperate to get the four of us through safely before a further rush of snow began again.

By some miracle, we passed up onto higher ground unscathed and began picking our way towards the cliff. As we approached, we realised that it was overhung with a vast serac – large, towering blocks of ice and snow reached out like fingers on a hand above us. Seracs are perilous to pass beneath as they are liable to drop off and crush you at any moment. Certainly, this was no place to pitch our tent for the night, but where else?

The temperature was now 30 below zero. Lew and I hunkered down, shouting to each other through the wind. We decided that our best chance was to head for the north ridge above us.

We moved diagonally across the steep snow face, which was, by now, bedecked with loose snow on top of old, hard ice. It felt precarious, as if it could all come away from the mountain in a single sheet at any moment. We reached the ridge in driving snow at about half past seven, in the dark. But this too was not as we had expected.

As I climbed up to the steepest part of the ridge, far from it having the rounded top that we had anticipated, I found myself looking straight down into space. This was a sheer ridge and I was perched on top of a cornice – an overhanging slab of snow and ice – and the last place I wanted to be.

Cornices are unpredictable, liable to "dinner plate" at any time – tilting and then flipping its occupants over the edge and into the abyss beyond. Lew came up behind me, closely followed by the other two young climbers. Now we had a choice: either we pitched the tent on the avalanche-prone slope we had just ascended or we tried to dig into the cornice.

We chose the latter option. We backed away from the cornice top and, using our ice axes, chipped away until we had created a ledge just big enough to accommodate one small tent. Nine inches from the outside peg was an abrupt 3,000-foot drop. It would have to do. With the storm closing in, all four of us bundled into the single tent.

We hadn't stopped all day, hadn't eaten and had long since run our water bottles dry. We slowly managed to get some food going, but cooking in a tent is a tricky business – the altitude slowed the boiling process and the steam condensed on the underside of the tent, showering small ice crystals down our necks as soon as one of us moved.

Trying to lie down was worse. Each of us was terrified about leaning too far to one side and taking the whole tent down the slope. Our only security was to rope ourselves up to a sling that we'd wrapped around a large rock. All of us were tied on, so if the tent did go, at least we'd be left hanging onto the rock and could try to save ourselves.

Barely anyone slept and by the early hours of the morning, it was clear our predicament hadn't got any better. The wind was no more forgiving than the day before. It bit and spat, trying to pull us from the ridge top, while the dreaded snow just kept on coming. There was no way we could attempt a descent in this.

With the prospect of another night up here, we agreed that we'd attempt to extend our little ledge out just enough to get another tent up and give ourselves more room.

We now had two tents facing each other on the top of the gentler side of the cornice; a sheer ice face beneath them. We shared out the last of the rations, which wasn't much, given that we hadn't anticipated being caught on the mountain for so long, and hunkered down.

It wasn't long after that that Steve Molloy, an enthusiastic, capable climber and the youngest of our team at just 18 years old, complained that his hands were beginning to swell. Both he and Steve Sands, were losing feeling in their fingertips and suspected it was frostbite.

Time was now of the essence, but there was little chance of rescue – this was 1986, there were no satellite phones and we were days from anywhere. We had to hope that the weather took a change for the better. But even if it did, I wasn't sure how these guys were going to make the 10-hour climb down with frostbitten fingers that were quickly turning black.

— • —

We had started on the road that would lead us to that moment on peak 6529 two years earlier. For any climber, the ultimate dream is to participate in a Himalayan expedition. This mountain range more than any other seems to hold a strange power for people and I was not immune – I'd been gazing up at them ever since I first put a poster of Mount Everest on my bedroom wall.

As I approached the age of 40, desperately seeking a positive escape from the bitter stresses of trying to run a London police station and feeling like I was getting nowhere, the Himalayan dream became a compulsion. The only way to free myself of it was to do it.

I found that there were a number of expeditions on the lookout for team members, but I doubted whether my modest skills on the rock would have been good enough to have joined one. Besides, I quickly decided that I didn't want to climb with strangers – I thought it would be far more interesting to put a team together and train them up from scratch.

I placed an advert in the police paper, *The Job*. It read: "Climbers with limited experienced wanted to take part in Himalayan expedition in 1986", and appeared, I think, below a request for Jimmy Shand memorabilia and a classified for a wooden train set. The result was an unexpected flood of 50 applicants from policemen all over London.

In a panic, I rang up Lew Hardy, a good friend and qualified mountain guide who was teaching sport science up at Bangor University in North Wales.

"Lew, how would you feel about leading a team of 50 climbers up a Himalayan peak somewhere?" I asked.

He swallowed hard. "What peak exactly do you want to climb?"

"That's where you come in!" I said.

Lew was friends with legendary Welsh climber, Mo Anthoine, and, after some consultation with Mo, identified a range of peaks suitable for an inexperienced, but well-trained, team. They were called Jogin and were in the Gangotri area of the Garhwal Himalaya in northern India.

73

"But there's no way we could take 50 men," said Lew. "So before we do anything else, you need to narrow the team to less than half the number you've got."

— • —

I told everyone what we would be letting ourselves in for. We would be climbing in areas where people had never been before, I said. In a hostile environment where, at the time, one in every eight climbers who went to the Himalayas didn't come back. I urged them to talk it through with their partners, because if they couldn't accept that possibility, they shouldn't go. The reality must have sunk in. By the following week, there were only 20 willing applicants left.

The next step was to get them climbing. I set up an exercise in the Dauphiné Alps with a view to testing their fitness, stamina and attitude. I wanted to make sure everyone had a say in the decision. So aside from trying to ascertain who was capable of learning to climb under strain at high altitude, I asked each person to pay attention to how well everyone else worked in the group.

This was really important, as far as I was concerned, because the whole team was going to have to live with each other at close quarters for three or four weeks at high altitude in basic conditions. Food would be bad, it would be hard work and there'd be a lot of down time when they weren't pushing for a summit. They had to be able to get on with each other.

The week in the Dauphiné was followed by a second test on the north face of Ben Nevis: four days of climbing in the depths of winter. We cracked off some really famous routes, all difficult, grade five climbs – with inspiring names like Zero Gully, Point Five and The Curtain – to really hone everyone's skills. By the time we were back in London, I had no doubt that the guys that were left had the capability to take on the Himalayas.

Not everyone was so sure. Before that final test in Scotland, one of the guys had contacted me to say he wanted to pull out. I'd been a bit shocked, as he was himself a qualified guide and a very good climber.

"I'm worried about what you're taking on here, John," he told me. "I've seen these guys and I'm not terribly sure they've got the training to do what you're asking them to do in the Himalayas."

He felt that what I was doing was actually quite dangerous and decided he didn't want to be a part of it.

This was a real shock to me. We were nearly a year into preparing for the trip by this point and this was the first time I'd heard that. I trusted our guide Lew with my life – and have done many times since – but to have such a good climber make a judgement like that made me very anxious.

I've since learnt that if you don't get a slap in the face in the early stages of an expedition, the alchemy for succeeding doesn't happen. After that comment, I got absolutely frantic about detail and scenario planning. Everything I thought that I had in place to keep people safe, I checked and rechecked – and then took extra precautions.

But I also trusted Lew. His knowledge and experience were far superior to my own, and he'd been there in the Dauphiné and again on the north face of Ben Nevis, where he'd not only sharpened the team's climbing skills, but also had them camping out in the snow in the wildest conditions. There was no one on the final climbing party of 18 that I would have chosen if he'd been against it.

Before I'd placed that advert in *The Job*, half the team had never climbed and only two of us had any alpine experience, but by the end of the two years, everyone was competent, though could hardly be described as experienced. Lew was to be climbing leader supported by an aspirant guide, Chris Parkin, while I would lead the expedition. In addition to the climbing party, we also had a base camp manager and medical officer, Dr Peter Savundra.

— • —

The Gangotri region, in which the Jogin range lies, is about 200 miles north east of Delhi, close to the Tibetan border, requiring a trip of about six weeks. Lew and I had formed a plan to attempt to get as many of the expedition members as possible up the southeast ridge of a peak called Jogin I, which, at 21,200 feet was also known as "The High Priestess". It had been climbed six times, but never by a British team. We also wanted to attempt the east ridge of Jogin II and have a go at the north-west face and north ridge of peak 6529 – neither of which had ever been climbed by anyone.

On 21 August 1986, we arrived at Delhi Airport in the early hours of the morning. We met Superintendent PM Das from the Indian police force, who would be the final climber making up our team, and picked up Trog Royle and John Robertson, two of our guys who had flown out earlier to wrestle our gear through customs. We'd been told that it was not unusual, at the time, for it to take three weeks to get freight out of New Delhi airport. After two years of planning and at least a week before we were into the Himalaya proper, we were desperate not to lose time.

We boarded the buses that would take us to Gangotri that morning. It was my first time in India and it was a wonderful experience as we worked our way up into more and more remote regions – though some of us came to find the precipitous mountain roads as frightening as the climbing itself. The higher we got, the more often we would find a landslide blocking the buses path, whereby we would have to get out and carry all our stuff over the rubble, eventually linking up with a bus on the other side that would take us deeper into the mountains.

Arriving in Gangotri three days later, we enlisted porters to help carry the expedition equipment and started a further three-day walk-in to base camp up at 15,400 feet. This is roughly 1,000 feet higher than the Matterhorn in Austria – a mountain that I had had to throw everything at to climb some years earlier. Here in the Himalayas, we would be starting our climbs from the height at which that iconic summit meets the sky.

Up we hiked, through dense forest to end of the tree line. Then came meadow land, where we caught our first full glimpse of the high mountains, followed by the rocky, medial moraine of the valley and finally, base camp, sitting above a large, pristine lake – Kedar Tal.

It was an awe-inspiring spot: clear and cold at night, it fortuitously caught the sun between nine o'clock and three o'clock every day before the cloud closed in. The snow seemed to cover only the peaks above 18,000 feet, leaving base camp mercifully clear, save on two or three occasions.

— • —

A proper look at Jogin II from base camp told us that it had little to recommend it. Not only was the line up to the peak uninspiring, but it was likely fraught with danger. It was riddled with patches of broken rock and the east ridge itself strewn with loose rock that would have involved scrambling for hours. We resolved to abandon it and instead focus on getting as many of the team up Jogin I as we had planned, then attempt peak 6529 – which was clearly the most difficult project – with a smaller team.

Between 6–10 September, we succeeded in putting 10 men on the summit of Jogin I in three teams. In the days leading up to the attempt, we had established three staging camps at 16,400 feet, 17,700 feet and 18,700 feet. From camp three, a long snow plod would then take you to the foot of The High Priestess's steep southeast ridge, which could then be climbed 1,000 feet to the summit.

The first team, led by our aspirant guide Chris Parkin, had made it to Camp Three before both Chris and Trog Royle became too ill with altitude sickness to make the final push for the summit. Faced with the possibility of the whole team having to withdraw, the young Steve Molloy, John Robertson and Trevor Barnes, who had no comparable experience climbing at altitude to speak of, chose to bravely go on alone.

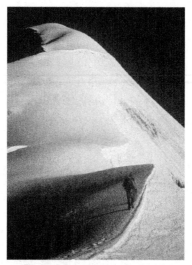

The long slog up from camp three to
the summit of Jogin 1.

Together, they made the first British ascent of Jogin I. It was wonderful that these apparent novices had successfully fought their way up the summit and, when we passed the team on our own ascent to Camp Three in the early afternoon of the following day, they were, rightly, on top of the world.

Resting at Camp Three that evening, awaiting our chance to make a bid for the summit at daylight, I was starting to get worried about one of my companions, Fraser Dodds. He'd grown quiet and withdrawn, and wouldn't take on any food. He was clearly suffering from altitude sickness, but probably didn't want to say anything that might jeopardise his chances of going to the summit. I couldn't blame him for that, but I was worried that if we were up here too long, there was a risk that he might develop a pulmonary oedema, where fluid starts to collect in the lungs.

The next morning, we set off on the long traverse through knee-deep snow. About 300 feet from the summit, Fraser was starting to look really rough. I urged him to consider calling a halt; that this was only going to get worse the higher he went. But he wouldn't be persuaded.

"I've got to go on, John, I've promised people I'll do this!" he said. "My local pub have even sponsored me free beer for three months after I get back. I've got to put their flag on top of the mountain!"

At the summit of The High Priestess (Jogin I) in the Himalayas. In total, we got 10 guys to the top of Jogin I in a first British Ascent in 1986.

Awe-inspiring views out from the
upper slopes of Jogin 1.

Knowing that if the worst came to worst, we could reach base camp in a day from Camp Three and that the effects of altitude sickness will subside quickly, if not prolonged, I conceded and we pushed on to the summit.

It was the first time that any of us had been part of a first British ascent and, here we were, walking where so few had set foot before, right up at 21,000 feet. We could see for miles. But we didn't hang around on the summit long… In all the pictures that I've got, we all look jubilant, but Fraser looks hollowed out. We got him down the mountain as quickly as we dared, which was a good job, because, by the start of the descent, he was frothing at the mouth.

Back at base camp, Fraser wasn't the only one in trouble. Chris Parkin had, by now, been diagnosed by our medical officer has having pleurisy, which he suspected had been picked up from flea bites. It was decided the best thing that he could do would be to descend to Gangotri and make his way home as soon as possible.

With Chris gone, two more climbers showing signs of pleurisy and a further three crippled by altitude sickness, base camp was getting restless. It was at this point that Lew and I decided that if anyone was going to have a crack at peak 6529, it needed to be the strongest climbers and that we ought to move quickly – climbing alpine-style, eschewing staging camps and carrying everything with us so as to be self-sufficient.

— • —

Steve Molloy and Steve Sands had jumped at the chance to have a go at 6529, but now, as we waited out the storm in our Gore-Tex tents – too thin for the battering that they were being asked to put up with – they were likely cursing their decision. Lew had determined that Steve Sands had developed frostbite in six fingers; Steve Molloy in nine. Our concern was that if the weather didn't change soon, their fingers might be in too bad a state to hold their ice axes on the downclimb.

That afternoon, I unzipped the tent door to look outside and review the weather.

"Hey Lew, I think the weather's improving you know!" I shouted.

He looked at me as if I was mad. "Why are you fooling yourself, John, you know it's not clearing up."

By now the zip had already gone up on the other tent.

"What's happening John?" came Steve's slightly excited voice.

"Lew thinks the weather's getting better!" I yelled.

"Do you reckon we'll be able to get off this mountain then?"

"Yeah, sit tight, but it's looking good."

As I zipped the tent back up, Lew looked over to let me know that he clearly thought this was an inappropriate strategy to be using. The benefits would be short lived if the weather really didn't change, but I knew I had to keep the guys' morale up to get them through another night on the ridge.

— • —

Dawn cracked beautiful and blue the next morning. Thank God, I thought, peering up at the sky. We helped the guys get dressed. We had to bind their ice axes onto their arms in case the lack of feeling in their fingers caused them to drop them – because if they dropped them, we were really in trouble. Both of them were wide-eyed and quiet, but bravely got on with it.

"We're getting off this mountain," I reassured them.

At seven o'clock, we began our retreat down the north-west face with Lew bringing up the rear. The first few pitches were frightening. After the past two days' weather, the snow hadn't had time to compact, leaving it loose and precarious. It was my job to make steps for the others to follow and I ploughed up to my knees until my feet found a solid layer below.

We made slow but sure progress and, by the sixth pitch, we were back in the gully that we had ascended on the way up. I had managed to get a rock peg in to give us some measure of security – things were looking up. But, by the time Lew arrived, the peg came out in his hand on the second pull. Knee-deep in the snow-filled gully, we had had enough and opted to abseil the next three pitches that would get us out onto the open ice face.

By midday, we had 2,300 feet to go. Just as we had on the way up, we now moved together in pairs, 150 feet apart. I would go down, down, down, then wait as the ice screws came whizzing along the rope as Lew swept them up on his way through. We climbed for a long, long day.

At one point, I was hanging on my ice axes, waiting for the ice screws to come down the line, and I must have fallen asleep. I woke up when my head dropped forward and banged against the ice.

Steve and Steve performed extremely well and managed to remove some 40 ice screws between them on the descent, as well as hold onto their axes. By nightfall at half past six, we had just 150 metres to go, so decided to keep pushing. Three hours later, we were back in the hanging valley where our ascent had started, tired but very grateful that everyone had made it.

We found some tea bags that we had left behind three days before and made a pot, then searched our pockets for scraps to ward off the hunger.

— • —

At four o'clock in the morning, I woke up and felt compelled to go outside and watch the sun rise. As I sat on a rock waiting for it to come up the valley, I had a deep, profound feeling of gratitude for being saved. When you're putting your arse on the line for your own sense of achievement, it's hard to pray for safety. You are in no position to ask for help when things go wrong – and yet, as I sat there, I kept asking myself why we had been allowed to live.

I turned it over in my mind as the sun melted the darkness of the valley. As it slowly revealed the ragged geometry of the peaks, I realised I'd had my fun out here for all these weeks – now I needed to get back to my wife and sons.

Gradually, I woke the others. Steve and Steve's frostbitten hands were starting to thaw out and the extent of the damage was becoming clear – they were now swollen up like black sausages. Lew and I dressed their hands as best we could and then, as a group, we made for the comparable luxury of base camp.

Our medic, Dr Peter Savundra, rushed to meet us. He ushered both men into the the inner section of our 12-foot square tent, while the other climbers set up small gas stoves to keep the tent heated to 38 degrees. Peter coated Steve and Steve's hands in new loose dressings of melolin and Sofra-Tulle, and gave them aspirin and a plethora of other drugs to increase circulation.

Within 24 hours, sensation in the form of burning paraesthesia returned, accompanied by blistering and loss of tissue – even their nails. Peter drained their blisters and washed their fingers in hydrogen peroxide, but we were now in a race against time to get off the mountain.

— • —

Not long after our epic climb on 6529, our 30 porters returned and we broke base camp. We'd been in the high mountains for several weeks and looked a lean, ragged bunch. I felt a potent mix of exhilaration, exhaustion and concern for our two guys with frostbite – particularly Steve Malloy. He was, at just 18 years old, among the most able climbers of us all and almost all of his fingers were frozen for their full length.

The three-day trek back to Gangotri took us through numerous mountain villages, one of which happened to be home to a local holy man and practitioner of Ayurvedic medicine. He met us on the trail one morning and, on finding out what had happen to the two Steves, asked if he could help us. I hesitated but Peter told me that there wasn't much he could do now – it was days yet to get back to Delhi and then England – and by the time that we got to the burns unit, who knows what might have happened. It was worth a try.

The holy man took us into a hut and unbound both the Steves' hands. He took out a pot of black goo that looked to me like axle grease (Peter later told me this was an Ayurvedic mixture of haldi, sodium nitrate and natural iodine) and carefully pasted it all over their hands, then bound them back up. He told them not to take it off until they got home.

From Gangotri, we pushed on to Delhi. We were coming down from the mountains, literally and metaphorically, and the three-day journey passed pleasantly – enlivened by a rest day in Uttarkashi, where we were feted by the whole town after playing (and losing to) the local football team.

We suffered somewhat from the heat of the lowlands and our footwear – some of us had to play in climbing boots – but mostly from the disorientation caused by being on a large, flat surface after a month in the Himalaya. By the time we reached Dehradun, the familiar walls of civilisation were starting to close back in on us. We found an old bar and had our first beer since leaving London.

— • —

Back home, at the burns unit in London, the two climbers' hands were recovering fast – much to the doctor's surprise. Thanks to Peter's excellent care and the Ayurvedic goo – which had succeeded in not only drying out their blisters but keeping their fragile hands free of insects – both men fully recovered without the loss of any digits.

Before we'd left on our expedition, I'd said in a local newspaper interview that in testing yourself against the elements, there must always be an element of risk. That risk had certainly presented itself. In addition to two severe cases of frostbite, three members of the team contracted viral infections that developed into pleurisy and three others suffered crippling altitude sickness. Yet, in all, 13 out of 17 climbers surmounted a Himalayan peak – 10 in a first-ever British ascent of Jogin I. But perhaps what was most remarkable was that we did it at all.

In his report for the *Alpine Journal* in 1986, Lew concluded that it had been "an unfashionably big, and yet outstandingly successful, expedition in a season of much failure and death" and that it was "most heartening that everyone came home in one piece". After all, in the valley adjacent to the one in which we had been climbing, the fatality rate had been 11 per cent.

Certainly, no conventional expedition would have let so many novices spread their wings in such a demanding area, and in the wake of the expedition, the Metropolitan Mountaineering Club went from strength to strength. Though there was a second expedition to attempt unclimbed peaks in the Karakoram Himalayas, I had passed the baton on to others by then.

It would have to be enough. I had spent my whole life in thrall to tales of the high mountains – finally, I had seen them for myself.

EIGHT
Returned

My reward for a safe return from the Himalayas was to take over as Divisional Commander at Stoke Newington Police Station. To my sadness, I found that my six-week absence had, in part, led to my Divisional Commander Roger Barr undergoing some sort of nervous breakdown under the pressure of work. He had gone off to recuperate, sadly never to return.

Roger was one of the finest leaders that I've ever met. He did everything wrong according to the national police leadership rulebook – and yet, to my mind, he did everything right. He was a wild, maverick guy, who enjoyed a drink and absolutely loved the men and women who worked for him. When the 1985 Tottenham riots were at their worst, he would sleep on an old prisoner's cell mattress on the floor of his toilet so that he was there for them if the wheels came off. In the end, it was his own wheels that came off. Now I would have to step into his shoes.

The situation in the London Borough of Hackney in 1986 was pretty grim. I found the mood in the station to be rather like Fort Apache. Stoke Newington Police Station had become notorious for allegedly heavy-handed dealings with local young black people, who despised the police, while many officers saw themselves as the last bastion of conservative values in an increasingly, and deeply threatening, anarchistic environment.

Far from being disreputable, many of the officers saw themselves as heroic – leading courageous sorties down the front line to the notorious haven of drug dealing that was Sandringham Road, whereupon their cars would be stoned by youths who saw the intrusion into their territory as aggressive and unnecessary.

This was a pretty desperate starting position for me as the new divisional commander. It wasn't long before I was struggling to manage the stresses of my new role, and it was taking its toll on my marriage. Hearing that I had very nearly lost my life in the Himalayas and that I had now returned with renewed vigour to work even harder and longer hours at the station had been the final straw for my wife Elaine. I'd left her in sole charge of our three young boys, and she had a full-time job herself running a high-street pharmacy. After six weeks away in the Himalayas, I found her on the edge of a nervous breakdown. She was beside herself with rage and despair, both extremes of which terrified me. She was worn out – and worn out of me going on adventures.

— • —

I didn't know where to turn. I heard somewhere about a weekend personal development course called "transpersonal psychology" and I was willing to try anything. It was held in a basement flat in Notting

Hill and involved a lot of meditation and drawing pictures as metaphors for your life. It was the kind of place that would have made my fellow officers wince, had I ever had the nerve to tell them about it, but it must have thrown up some interesting insights for me because it prompted me to ask the person who ran the course if she could recommend a good counsellor.

I found counselling could be as personally gruelling as climbing any mountain. But it was also punctuated with insightful experiences and, at times, moments of unbridled liberation. Inevitably, at some stage, we came to look at my relationship with my mother and father. The influence of having being brought up in the shadow of an angry mother and grandmother, and, much as I love them now, with two older sisters who were at times bossy and high on control, had left an impact on me: I found it hard to deal with conflict, particularly with women.

Like my father, I had learned that the safest path was one of 'avoidance'. Rather than face up to what was in front of me, escape and evasion became my coping mechanisms – whether it was sidestepping an argument, or taking off into the mountains for weeks at a time. Needless to say that much of what I was now struggling to deal with was the backlash of this lifelong strategy.

Elaine, too, had grown up with conflictual parents and both of us had been determined that we wouldn't be like that when we got married. But my inability to face up to things and vent my anger – and Elaine's frustration at not being able to connect with this dormant part of me – was leading us into the type of relationship that we had tried so hard to avoid.

— • —

Each of us have deeply ingrained fault lines that never really disappear, and we are all susceptible to dropping back into our old patterns. We can only hope to become more aware of them and their triggers, so that we have time to make useful choices rather than being a prisoner of our past experiences. But through the counselling process, which took years, I learnt to open up – to face up to my mother, my sisters and my wife in a healthy way – and Elaine and I rebuilt our marriage into something that has endured ever since. Likewise, my relationship with my two sisters is very special to me now.

I look back now with some shame and embarrassment about those days and the way that I ignored Elaine's and the boys' needs at that time. As I look at her now, and I still see the young girl that I first met who loved me so deeply, it grieves me that my love affair with the mountain caused her so much pain at that time in her life.

The truth is, when you make the choice to do one of these expeditions, it's a very selfish choice. It leaves a huge void behind for people who are having to sit and wait for you to return, and a lot of anxiety over whether or not you will return at all. I have to ask myself now how reasonable that was.

One wonders sometimes if it is a sense of inadequacy that drives people to take risks. But actually what I see time and again, watching people in my teams, is that when people come back they are closer to their feelings and emotionally closer to their loved ones – as a result of the experiences they've had. When you're up against it in these remote places, you do have some very profound moments.

I cry at times when I'm in my tent – particularly when I'm listening to music. Everything is heightened, accentuated. Life stops for you: you're not doing anything else. You don't need to worry about whether you've changed the oil in the car, or the mortgage. You don't have to worry about anything other than the mountain – and it's pretty obvious what you've got to do there. If you surround yourself with good guys who you trust to make sound judgements, then there is often a lot of solo time to reflect on people back home. You become profoundly thoughtful about them.

At the gravest moment on 6529, when it really looked like we wouldn't make it, the one thing that fired me up to keep going was the thought of getting back to my sons, and that warm afterglow stayed with me.

The realisation for me on coming out the other side of the Himalayas was that if I was going to continue to take people on expeditions, I'd want to be able to make sure they were supported before and during the expedition, of course, but also when they came back. I'd want to spend some time with them unpacking their experiences, helping them to make sense of them in a way that was going to be some benefit to them and the people around them for the rest of their life. It left me thinking that, if you're going to put in the hard work, time, money and risk that something like a big adventure requires, you should only do it if you can make some sense of it at the end.

— • —

When Elaine and I first got married, and she got her student grant through, she bought me a climbing rope. I will never forget that moment of kindness when she knew that I would inevitably be using it on dangerous exploits. When people sometimes say to me now, why do you do all these dangerous things? I often say, "Because I can". That is largely because I have Elaine to look after my mental health before, during and after adventures. My advice to anyone contemplating serious adventure is that your life will be a lot easier and richer if you have a good base camp behind you. Elaine has always been mine.

With my wife, Elaine.

NINE

Fathers And Sons

In the June of 1989, I woke up one morning to the realisation that my relationship with my father was shallow and guarded. I had really adored him as a boy and would have gladly followed him over a cliff, but now I was 43 and he had a frustrating obsession with trying to manage my career in the police in a way that would tick all of the right boxes for himself. This was unsurprising given his own prominent position within the force – he was one of Her Majesty's Inspectors of Constabularies, responsible for inspecting the police itself – but the pomp and ceremony, the hierarchy and rules that were so important to him, were not what fired me up.

As Elaine and I got deeper into counselling to save our marriage, I realised that this too need to be confronted. The job seemed to be somewhere at the root of the problem, so I decided that the only way to do this was in neutral territory. I took the bull by the horns and called my dad at home.

"Why don't you come away with me for a weekend in the Lake District?" I said.

He sounded a bit taken aback – he was in his early 70s at the time – but he agreed nonetheless. He immediately offered to book up a hotel room for the pair of us. I told him that we weren't going to stay in a hotel, that I wanted us to go camping in the mountains.

"But I haven't got any kit," he said.

"Don't worry about that, I'll take care of all the kit for both of us," I told him.

He must have realised how important this was to me because, in all fairness to him, he never made the slightest protest after that.

— • —

I drove up to Nottingham to pick him up. He was standing on the doorstep with my mother when I arrived: both of them looking rather nervous. I got him settled into the car and in no time at all he was asking me how I was getting on at work.

"I'd really appreciate it if we could not talk about work in any way for the next two days," I said. "Can we do that?"

He looked shocked, but said he would try, and we settled into silence. It was unfamiliar territory for two so-called extroverts to find themselves in. The trouble was that we knew no other way to communicate, and that awkward silence stayed with us all the way to Cumbria.

We arrived at our destination in Haweswater around two o'clock. I had run in these mountains many times and knew the area well. It is a remote wilderness, unique in that, for the Lakes in spring, there are rarely any walkers to be seen. We got changed into hiking clothes and boots and I gave him a rucksack to carry, already loaded with camping gear.

It was a beautiful, warm afternoon with a long, light evening ahead of us – I couldn't have asked for better conditions. As we set off up into the hills, I asked my father to tell me about his life. I listened for hours, absolutely fascinated. It was as if the landscape had given him space and he was opening up, expanding to fill it. I was getting to know a whole a different side of him.

— • —

He had been born in Shanghai in 1916, where his father, my grandfather, worked for the Colonial Police Force. On the day that he was born, it was a celebrated date in the Chinese calendar. That, coupled with the fact that it was snowing in Shanghai that day and that he was born with red hair, meant he was declared a "Lucky Joss".

"The servants thought I was some sort of deity, so they would bring gifts and people to see me," he told me.

I laughed gently as I heard this story now, remembering that whenever he would tell this story to guests at the dinner table, my mother would always be quick to tell them, "Yes, and every day, I have to have drag him back down to Earth and remind him that he's only an ordinary mortal like the rest of us!"

He had grown up with his younger brother and sister in Shanghai, whom he adored and who clearly adored him, until, at the age of seven, he was sent to boarding school in England – the same school that I would later go to. This was in the days of the proverbial "slow

97

boat to China" and, since there was no time to travel between England and China in a school holiday, he was only to see his parents twice in the next eight years – being brought up instead by aunts and uncles.

Unlike me at that age, he seemed to have taken this absence of his parents in his stride and maintained that he had had a happy life as young boy. He had been a great sportsman and was, he said, never happier than when back at school or on the games field. After a stint in the RAF during the war, he had gone on to a distinguished career in the police force.

Our lives had seemed to follow such similar paths; in no small part, I supposed, because I had chosen to follow him. And yet here we were, wildly different people trying to find common ground.

— • —

At around six o'clock, we reached the top of a crater-like ridge and set off down a sheep track to a hanging valley below, where I planned for us to camp for the night. My father was starting to get tired and, much to my astonishment, I saw that he was frightened of the steep, rocky inclines. For the first time ever, I held his hand, helping him down the mountain until we reached a small lake at the bottom of the crater. I put the tent up and left to him to rest while I cooked our dinner on the gas stove.

We drank whisky and ate our food, and marvelled at the view as evening sun went down. He had never done anything like this before, he told me, and as I tucked him up in his sleeping bag that night, his look of wide-eyed innocence reminded me of my own son on our first camping trips together.

The next morning, I made us a light breakfast and we broke camp. Something had happened that night that transformed our relationship forever. We walked down that mountain like two good friends. He never asked me about my career again, whatever the ups or downs. In fact, my sisters – who had often said to me in the past that I was taking on tough challenges in order to prove something to him – tell me I became something of a hero to him that weekend, and that he loved to tell his friends about my latest adventures.

I'm not so sure I had anything to prove, but I certainly loved to see the look of excitement when I told him stories of my latest epic in some far-off place. I could see that he would have loved to have done the same himself and I was glad to know that this brought him happiness in his twilight years.

My relationship with my own three sons has been transformed by the various adventures that we've shared together in remote parts of the world. For me, it is always a chance to get to know them better as people. I doubt, by now, that there is much that they don't know about my own life, as we are always chatting and exchanging stories when we're away, perhaps even more so than when we meet on familiar ground.

— • —

Some 17 years after that weekend away, I had to break the news to my dad that I was intending to row across the Atlantic. He was 87 and we were on the beach at Llanbedrog in North Wales on a family holiday. Far from being concerned, as I had expected, he said, "Are you going alone or with a partner?"

I told him that I planned to row with a partner, but hadn't decided who to ask yet.

"I'll come with you John, I can row!"

Having prepared myself to have to assure him of my own safety, I now found myself having to quietly let him down.

"You're a bit too old for this one I'm afraid, Dad".

But I didn't doubt for a second that he'd meant it.

My dad raises a cup of whisky for the camera from his tent in Haweswater – a weekend that would change our relationship forever.

TEN

London To Paris By Boat

People sometimes ask if there is anything you would have done differently. We can probably all think of profound responses to this question, but the one that always springs to mind for me, is that I would like to have gone to a school that did rowing. I think I would have really enjoyed rowing.

I was in my mid-40s before I'd ever picked up a proper oar. I was on a training course at Wolfson College, Cambridge and for three months, at six o'clock every morning, I had the opportunity to go rowing. I absolutely loved the feeling of making a boat fly fast with a group of guys all pulling together. When it goes, it really goes and I found this terrifically exciting.

One weekend during those three months, I went away to Paris with my wife. We were in a coach driving alongside the Seine in Versailles and I looked across the river at the view – and suddenly I was transported to a moment years ago in a race.

"I've just remembered something," I said. 'I've got to row up that river."

"What are you talking about?" she replied.

It had all come flooding back to me, I explained. We'd been hit by storm during the Scottish Islands boat race and had been forced to shelter in a bay. We sat there for hours until we got to dreaming about the adventures that we really wanted to do. One of mine had been to row from London to Paris. I had imagined us pulling up the Seine towards the imagined finish, and now here I was in Paris. Even back at work the following week, I couldn't let the thought drop.

It would great be fun, I thought, to take a team of police officers out in an old whaler rowing boat. Not a sleek, fancy rowing boat but something Shackleton might have had to use. I imagined that we would start outside the Houses of Parliament, then row down the Thames and out into the Channel, eventually turning south towards the mouth of the Seine and up to Paris.

As luck would have it, my duties as a Chief Superintendent at the time included administrative responsibility for the police unit that looked after the River Thames. Having sketched my idea out only roughly, I decided to confide in one of the officers that worked in the unit. He didn't think I was barking mad, which was a start, but suggested that I should get a feel for the river, and invited me to come out on the Commissioner's launch to see the start of the Tall Ships Race, which was scheduled to depart on the Thames within the next few days.

Sure enough, I took up his kind offer and found myself enjoying cruising around these magnificent tall ships, their masts competing with the towers of the City skyline. At some stage, the Inspector in charge of the launch noticed the arms of Tower Bridge opening up to let the ships through. He suggested we follow and I readily agreed.

But as we passed under the bridge, a loud clanging noise came from above and one of the bridge arms dropped well below where it should have been. Clearly, there was something wrong and we were left bobbing about in the boat while we waited for the arm to be ratcheted back up.

"This is typical of my husband," said my wife Elaine to one of the other passengers, "he's talking about rowing from London to Paris, but he can't even get under Tower Bridge without breaking it!"

This passenger turned out to be an entrepreneur called David Kay. He was the kind of man who had flown helicopters on James Bond movies and it would turn out, was one of life's great fixers.

"Is your husband really going to row across the Channel?" he asked.

Elaine told him that I was and he started to ask her how I thought I was going to get the money to undertake something like that.

"I have no idea, but he's sitting over there if you want to ask him," she said.

He walked towards me at the other end of the launch and we started chatting. At this point, I had no more than an extremely vague plan, and no idea where I was going to get the money from, or even where to find an old whaler to row. But he seemed unperturbed, telling me to leave it to him and he would see if he could help us. I had a hip flask of whisky on me and I shared some with him as we talked, but as the bridge arm was finally cranked back up and we left the boat that evening, I never thought I'd see this stranger again.

Late the following morning, I received a phone call. To my

surprise, it was David. After the whisky the previous day, he wanted to check if I was really serious about rowing from London to Paris. When I told him I was, he said, "How much will you need to get the project off the ground?"

To be honest, I had no idea, but said that I assumed it would be around £10,000. I waited for a sharp intake of breath on the other end of the line but he didn't baulk at that. Instead, he asked, "Would a champagne company be all right to sponsor the expedition, like Pol Roger Champagne?"

Taken aback, I said that sounded pretty good.

"I presume you'll need a whaler rowing boat or two, and in terms of your support vessel, would a Royal Navy minesweeper do the job?"

I was open-mouthed at the end of the phone. Who was this guy? I garbled yes, and he told me he'd fix it.

— • —

True to his word, David Kay got Pol Roger to sponsor us, got us the boats and, though not quite a minesweeper, a Royal Navy reserves support vessel to follow our progress through the channel.

Now I needed a team.

A few test runs with a whaler rowing boat against the flood tide in the Thames was enough to suggest to me that this was going to be really hard work. I'd figured out that the best strategy might be to have four crews that we would rotate in and out of the boat, as if on a continuous relay, two hours on, four hours off.

It was going to be necessary to handpick some people who could be trained up to row these things. We wanted the fastest crews but they had to be able to get on with each other given the strain of the task required and the amount of time they would be spending together in a small space. Pol Roger had also bought into it being a police expedition, so everyone had to be a police officer.

I put out another advert in *The Job* and within a week had more than enough interested responses. I'd need to whittle the list down. So I sent everyone the same message asking them to meet me at a certain spot in Hounslow, south-west London, at eight o'clock one night. I didn't give them any more details, but assured them they would be back in time for work the next morning.

That night, at the Public Order Training Centre in Hounslow, everyone on my list turned up. They jumped into the minibuses that I'd hired and we drove down to a Royal Navy training facility down on the south coast, where the last of the old whaler rowing boats in the country were kept. The Navy used these boats for training exercises and the facility was run by a right old sea dog. I'd arranged for him to get everyone out on the sea in the dark, racing each other in these boats.

The sea was choppy that night and some of the men found it quite spooky to be out on the waves with only an overcast moon. It was one o'clock in the morning by the time that we brought everyone back on shore and our host had laid on what he called a "pot mess": essentially, a big white china cup of soup – a greasy grey soup that looked a bit like vomit – and a big chunk of bread. These cups were passed round and most of the men had a go at the stuff, which they found tasted far better than it looked. At the end of what had been a long, hard session, I asked my friend John Robertson to do a whip-round and get a fiver from everyone as a small token for the old sea dog who'd looked after us that night. John disappeared to gather the money.

When he came back, he told me that a few of the men had refused to cough up. I asked why and he told me they didn't think the soup was worth a fiver. I told him to go back and tell them that I expected them to do it as a mark of our friendship and gratitude, whether they thought it was worth it or not. When several of the the officers still refused to pay, I asked him to scribble down their names for me.

It was four o'clock in the morning when we eventually got back to Hounslow. I told everyone I wanted them back at work that day. There was to be no time off. Later that morning, I wrote to all of the guys who had refused to pay the money the night before and explained that I was cutting them from the team. If they really couldn't put their hand in their pocket to give a fiver to someone, if they'd found that small sacrifice too difficult, they hadn't seen anything yet. The challenge out at sea would be much greater.

Some of these officers were head honchos in the public order division, tough-looking blokes, and they were gutted. But I knew that the essence of a good team was when people were prepared to make sacrifices whether or not there was anything coming back, not people who would constantly be measuring the cost of things. Our rowers would be training at the crack of dawn for six months. We were going to have row more than 480 miles, much of it at sea. I was interested in the ones who showed total commitment from the outset and who didn't mind how hard it was.

— • —

As we moved on with our planning, we decided to try to raise a substantial amount of money for a charity called Fight for Sight, based at Moorfields Hospital for people who couldn't afford to have the eye treatment that they needed. To do this, we needed to build up a bit of a profile, so we decided to stage a publicity stunt. We arranged for a photographer to come out on the Thames and take pictures of some of the crew in their police uniforms rowing one of the whalers past the Houses of Parliament.

But the morning that the photograph was due to be taken, I got a telephone call from the photographer. He was concerned about how safe it was to shoot, given the severe weather warning that day that was predicting hurricane force winds gusting in from the south west. Surely, the crew wouldn't be going out in this, he said.

I told him that these rowing boats were originally used for hunting whales and designed for Atlantic swells. Well, what about him, he wanted to know.

"You'll be strapped into a life jacket in the Commissioner's launch. It's impossible for those launches to sink," I assured him.

With a bit more persuasion, he agreed that it could turn out to be the shot of lifetime and the nearest that he would ever get to shooting in such conditions at sea.

That morning the snapper reluctantly set off in the launch and, in no time at all, he was sick as a dog. He clung on for dear life as the wind sucked the water out of the river, constructing towers that spiralled around him as the launch ploughed through the waves to find the perfect spot to get the photograph. But amid all this chaos, he got his shot and it turned out to be worth it.

The following day, his picture appeared in the front page of *The Times* and made the *Sunday Times* supplement the following weekend. It went on to feature in *Life* magazine, *Paris Match* and a number of other famous publications – in fact, *Life* chose it as one of their most famous pictures ever. I was told he'd made more than £60,000 in the first week from selling that shot.

Our publicity stunt outside the Houses of Parliament for the London to Paris row ended up with this photo making the international press, including *Life* magazine. Credit: Rex/Nils Jorgensen.

As for the men in the boat, the majority of them never went to sea again, such was the alarming nature of the waters that day. There was only one person sitting in the boat who was truly excited by the experience. Dave MacDonald would not only help me to take the crew from London to Paris, but also would subsequently lead the first-ever row around Great Britain, row the whole of the west coast of the California and, later, become my business partner for 10 years. That experience on the Thames was a turning point from which he went from strength to strength.

— • —

With a solid half-a-year's worth of training under our belts, sponsorship from a prestigious champagne brand and with money on the books for Fight for Sight providing that we could deliver the goods in Paris, we set off in May 1990 down the Thames. We had planned more or less a direct line from Dover across the Channel to Le Havre, but, inevitably, after hauling hard for a day and night, we found ourselves blown of course and having to track down the French coast to find the Seine estuary.

After relatively smooth conditions in the Channel proper, we were making good time – with each team rowing solidly for two hours before being relieved and swapping on to the support vehicle for some respite.

But the big seas off the north coast of France were turning out to be the toughest part of the row. The waves were building as they were coming into shore, knocking the boat about and giving all on board cause for concern that the boat would roll over as we struggled to make progress. Thankfully, the provenance of the whalers held up far better than our nerves: they were bulky as hell and hard work, but they had been built to weather the worst. Eventually, and to everyone's relief, we pulled into the mouth of the Seine and camped up for the night.

The next morning, as we waited for the tide to change so that we could ride the big wash of water up the river, we were clowning around, looking for things to do to pass the time. Some of the crew started making a video of the fun, for the benefit of which, as senior officer, I was made to walk the plank off our support vessel which, though supposedly a Navy vessel, bore closer resemblance to *The African Queen*.

As I was sploshing about in the water beneath the boat, the river police, *Les Gendarmes de la Brigade Fluviale*, suddenly appeared. They hoiked me out of the water and asked us what the hell we thought we were doing. I tried to explain that it was just a bit of fun and that, in fact, we were police officers ourselves. But my attempt to play the police card was met with scant enthusiasm, and my tale about us having just rowed from London in a whaler was met with total disbelief.

"How are you going to get from here to Paris then?" they asked.

I replied plainly that we were just going to row there.

"But how will you get through all the locks?" they pressed, with confused looks on their faces.

"Oh, I didn't know there were locks, "I said sheepishly. "Is there a key or something?"

At this point, the *gendarmes* fell about laughing. It turned out that the locks on the Seine were about 100 yards wide. Huge great things that only open to allow big ships through. How had we masterminded the expedition this far and yet overlooked such a huge obstacle?

I was starting to wonder quite how we were going to make it up river; the *gendarmes* now wanted to come aboard and see our charts and I wasn't altogether sure we had any. At that point, our captain emerged from below deck in full naval regalia and, to everyone's surprise, broke into impeccable French. We're saved, I thought. He duly unzipped his smart naval briefcase to fetch our charts and pulled out the Bartholomew Road Atlas to France!

The French police looked absolutely horrified. My face dropped. Time seemed to slow down. And then people started laughing. I can only think that such was the ridiculousness of our situation that they decided in that moment that having come this far, they might as well as help us finish our journey. And they did. The *gendarmes* waited with us until the tide turned and accompanied us all the way up the Seine, even opening the locks through the night to let the crew row on.

— • —

It's 232 miles from Le Havre to Paris and we were making phenomenal progress. Two hours on, four hours off, we kept at it until we were well ahead of schedule. So much so, in fact, that we were going to have to hold up so as not to upset the official welcome party that had been arranged for us at the Eiffel Tower.

The Metropolitan Police Deputy Commissioner, the police band, our sponsors, even President Chirac's deputy was supposed to be turning up.

But now there was a lot of muttering going on.

"Boss, can we get in tonight?" the crew kept asking me. They knew we were flying and were keen to set a fast record; this was the first time anyone had done this after all.

As we got ever closer, one of my colleagues came up to me on the support vessel and asked if he could have a private word.

There was a lot of dissent in the camp, he said. "The guys aren't happy that I might hold everyone up just for the sake of publicity."

"What are you suggesting then?" I asked.

"I don't think it matters what decision you make, John, " he replied, "but just make it and tell them now, or they'll mutter forever."

I called everyone together, even the crew who were still rowing.

"Well done guys, we're on a fantastic time here. I'm conscious that there's a feeling among you that you want to go straight through and finish the race tonight. I'm going to tell you that's not going to happen. That's not going to happen because we've got a lot of people who've sponsored this trip and who've actually put themselves out for us, and we're not going to leave them high and dry. That's my firm and final decision, and you are going to have to accept it."

They looked down, crestfallen. Then I said: "However, if, under the cover of darkness, a crew were to set off and get under the Périphérique just short of the Eiffel Tower, then we will be able to take that as our finishing time. But that crew will have to get there and back without anyone seeing them."

This, they loved – and duly did. A small group snuck up river in the dark that night and set a time that other expeditions would struggle to beat – for a while at least.

— • —

The next day we lined up and ceremoniously rowed through to the centre of Paris as the band played and the dignitaries waved. We achieved what we set out to do and even made the national papers. To this day, I can replay the night-long, euphoric celebrations after we arrived in Paris. The men were some of the happiest people I have ever seen that night.

When I think back now, it was never really about me getting from London to Paris in a rowing boat. It was about me getting a team of guys together to do it, because I just knew it was going to be great fun. I couldn't believe that nobody had done it before; plenty of people did after us, of course, each of them improving on our effort and inching forward of our record.

ELEVEN

Muzungu

A quiet, modest young man sat across from me. He looked unsure of himself, as if he might make a dash for the door at any moment.

"How serious are you about doing something really worthwhile, Phil?" I asked him.

"I'm very serious," came the reply, quickly.

"And how hard are you prepared to work at this?" I said.

"I'm not afraid of hard work – I'll do whatever it takes."

I paused. "OK Phil, I've got just the project for you. You're going to go to a small village in the south west of Uganda called Rukungiri. Once there, you're going to seek out a couple of missionaries called Alice and John Tumesimi. They'll take you in to stay with them for as long as it takes you to build a school on a patch of land above their village."

He reeled back in his chair in shock. "But I don't know anything about building, let alone building in Uganda!" he said, his voice finding conviction for the first time.

"Well, you're going to need to start learning fast," I said, "but don't worry, when you get there you will find what you need on site."

He went quiet for a while. I could almost hear his brain trying to come to terms what I'd just asked him to do. He was only 19 after all.

Eventually, he stood up, looked me in the eyes with a deep, strong look, that I would later come to know well, and said, "I'll do it."

— • —

The series of events that had led to that meeting with Phil in my office in Scotland Yard started with a chance encounter shortly after our record-breaking London to Paris row some years earlier.

Pol Roger, the champagne company that had sponsored us, had asked me to join them for a soirée at an art exhibition that they were sponsoring in London. I accepted the invitation, but turned up feeling like a bit of a spare part, having no real interest in art myself. Fortunately, a young man, who turned out to be a salesman for Pol Roger, recognised me and struck up a conversation about our expedition.

"You're lucky to have had all these adventures," he said after we'd been talking for a while.

"Well, what about you," I asked. "Ever done anything like that yourself?"

He seemed a bit taken aback that I'd asked, and quickly brushed it off.

"No, not me, that," he said.

"Well have you ever dreamed of doing anything like it," I pushed.

He went quiet for a moment, before saying wistfully, "There is one thing that I would love to do – climb the Mountains of the Moon."

The name alone was enough to pique my interest.

"They sound incredible – where are they?"

He told me that they were in Uganda, on the border with Zaire. He had grown up in old colonial Kenya and that sometimes he and his parents would travel down to the Ugandan border from which you could see the Mountains of the Moon. Occasionally, the mist over the summits would clear and he would be able to see snow-capped peaks.

"Go on," I said, hooked.

The approach to the mountains was through thick elephant grass that covered the savannah at their base. That was where the ascent started. First came lush rainforest with giant trees, several hundred feet high; then came the Great Bigo Bog, where you would have to jump from tussock to tussock to avoid falling in. It was here, he declared, that there were giant earthworms, two feet long, that would spit poisonous venom into your eyes and blind you if you got too close.

If you crossed the bog safely, you would enter a vast open area with giant heather and lobelia plants, 20 feet high. Then came a ridge of steep rocks, which required careful climbing with ropes, until you reached a snow and ice field. There, you would need ice axes and crampons to make the final push to the summit.

His eyes were alight as if in a trance as he told me this account, all of it meticulously researched and memorised.

"But you've never been there?" I asked.

"No."

He said it in such a resigned way that it was clear that he never would either.

As the tube rattled me home to Essex, that night, I thought to myself, "He might never climb those mountains, but one day I will."

Not long after, I found myself bouncing around in the back of a minibus on a Highland pass in Scotland. I was on a climbing trip with Lew Hardy again and a buddy of his – Ray Wood, who was a successful mountaineering photographer. I'd asked Ray if he'd ever come across the Mountains of the Moon. Funnily enough, he said, he'd written an article about them in a previous issue of *The Climber and Rambler* magazine. He offered to send it to me.

The day that the envelope from Ray arrived, I was sat reading it in my lounge, when my eldest son Marcus came in. He was 17 at the time and looking over my shoulder, asked me if I was going on another expedition. I told him that I might be, but I hadn't decided yet.

"You always take everyone else on expeditions," he said, "I wish you'd take me."

I thought for a minute and then said, "All right, I'll take you, but on one condition: you'll have to lead it."

— • —

With Marcus and his mates involved, there was scope for the trip to be about much more than just climbing a mountain. The Mountains of the Moon is how ancient people referred to what are now called the Rwenzori (rainmaker) Mountains, and, in 1992, many of the communities surrounding them were only now emerging from the shadow of decades-long war.

With my eldest son Marcus in the Mountains of the Moon in 1992.

Through connections with the local church, we made contact with schools in the Fort Portal area and set about gathering enough books, science equipment and tools to fill an entire room of our house. These were dispatched ahead of us in a shipping container and we would pick them up on our arrival to distribute to the schools, before making our attempt on our chosen summit, Mount Stanley.

With such a long trip ahead of us, Elaine and I had taken our youngest son out of school to come with us. While, Marcus and I led the group up the mountain, Elaine and Julian, who was only nine at the time, took a long and rickety bus ride to stay with a couple that we met through the church.

Alice and John Tumesimi lived in something of a one-horse town called Rukungiri, way down in the south west of Uganda. When Elaine eventually found them, they were amazed that she had made such a perilous journey alone, much of the final leg having been crammed into the back of an old, open-back pickup with chickens and stern-looking men. When I finally joined them a week or so later, I was nothing if not a little embarrassed that I had let her make the trip alone – though deeply proud of her for having made it at all.

The Mountains of the Moon had proved to be everything that the Pol Roger salesman had predicted. But now, here in Rukungiri, the elation was beginning to subside. On my second day in the village, Alice took us to a small patch of wasteland on a hill overlooking the village. It was in a sorry state; nevertheless, Alice beamed as she told us how she had finally raised enough money to buy this land, declaring that it would, in time, be the site she had chosen for her school and for the workshop that John ran with the local prison. We walked down the opposite side of the hill to the one we had come up, between the rows of the banana plantation and a straggled collection of mud huts.

Everywhere that we looked there were young, naked children peering at us from around the doorway entrances. All with big eyes and regarding us with serious, silent countenances. But there were no mothers or fathers to be seen. These were the orphans of those who had died of AIDS, which had ravaged the country unchecked. The only adults here were care-worn, tired-looking grannies, doing what they could to look after the children, who would otherwise be left to fend for themselves. In some instances, young children were left to feed and look after the babies, explained Alice. Her school, when she could afford to build it, would be for these orphans.

Elaine and I were deeply moved by what we saw. We left Alice and John with some money, but it felt paltry compared to the struggle that they faced to get their project off the ground. I promised them that, one day, we would try to find them some help – though I had no idea how.

— • —

That opportunity presented itself when Phil came to see me that evening at the station. His father, John Grieve, who is perhaps one of the most well-respected detectives that the police force has ever known, had told me that Phil wanted to go travelling, but wasn't interested in the usual circuit. He wanted to leave something of value in the place he visited. I think he thought I would recommend Operation Raleigh – the main adventure gap-year outfit at the time – but the more I heard about Phil, the more I thought that he had something else to him.

A couple of months went by after my first meeting with Phil and, occasionally, I would get a visit to update me on his progress. He was working in a pub in the evening to earn money and during the day, he was attending various college classes on bricklaying, plumbing and electricity while he got a plan together in his head about how he was going to build this school. Within six months, he assured me he had it all together. I gave him the route to Rukungiri, and he was off.

Much to my surprise, he appeared back in my office only a few weeks after he'd left. He looked desolate.

"It was terrible, John. Every time you want something you have to travel all the way to the capital to get it. That takes all day. Every time you give money to someone, you never see the goods. The water pump nearby isn't working and, to cap it all, Alice and John are born-again Christians and want me to keep joining them in prayers. I'm not a born-again Christian!"

As he got more worked up telling me his tale of woe, I couldn't help but laugh and, fortunately, that seemed to relax him a bit.

That, evening we met again and sat down, determined to make a new plan. We talked through all the various scenarios that he'd encountered and that could crop up again, and looked at how he might get over them a second time around. He had been left some money by his grandmother, he said, and now decided he would put that into the project.

As he was about to leave my office that night, I stopped him at the door.

"Phil, I have 100 per cent confidence in you pulling this off. Get out there and don't come back again until the job is done."

I believed it and hoped that he would ring me up for advice while he was over there, but several months went by and I'd heard nothing. I would get the odd update from his father, but little about how he was or his progress. I began to worry.

— • —

When I first looked up from desk to greet the person at the door, I had assumed it to be one of the heavyset constables at the station. It took me a moment or two to register that it was Phil.

"I bloody did it," he said with a huge grin on his face.

I was gobsmacked. This was wasn't the Phil I had last seen, this was a man. I immediately reached over the table to shake his hand.

It transpired that the first thing that he tried to do when he got back to Rukungiri was fix the water pump. He could find nobody with plumbing skills who seemed to want to do anything about it, so decided to take the thing apart himself.

Having worked out that the main problem seemed to be a rubber washer, he'd travelled to the capital, Kampala, and managed to find one in a back street shop. He'd fitted it and got the pump working again.

That evening, there was a large queue of women lining up to fill their water containers. Before that they had had to walk five miles every time that they needed to collect fresh water. As he'd looked on, surprised at the seemingly big impact that his day's work had achieved, something in him clicked.

By the time Phil left for England, he had built the first section of the school and children were starting to come down the hill to their first class. As I sat there listening to him excitedly rattle off his story, I noticed how much of a profound change those months away had had upon him.

— • —

Some years later, a friend of my son Marcus, who now ran a charity in Uganda called the Rwenzori Foundation, had come back from a trip to Rukungiri. He recounted a tale that local people had told him about a *muzungu* (white man) who had appeared from nowhere and in just a few months, had built a school. With that, he had left and the locals had never seen him again.

When Alice and John Tumesimi next came to England on a fundraising tour, we hosted a big dinner in celebration of their visit and invited the mystery muzungu, Phil Grieve – who by then was training as a paramedic in London.

We were at our house – which my sons and their friends affectionately call "The Dukes" – when Alice clapped her hands with joy and rushed to give Phil a great cuddle. He looked suitably embarrassed, but had a tear in his eye when she opened out a long picture of the Rukungiri school, now made up of many buildings and housing several hundred paying students. The whole project now funds her AIDS orphans from the nearby plantation settlement, who all go there for free.

TWELVE
An Old Ghost

When I was very young, my sisters, as most elder siblings do, used to tell me I was stupid. I certainly wasn't as intellectually gifted as they were and, since I couldn't compete, I ended up playing the joker. I grew up thinking I didn't really deserve to do particularly well at school and when, halfway through my A levels, my father said that I could leave school and get a job, it seemed to me at the time that I was being set free. The reality was that I left school with just a handful of GCSEs and never really had a chance to prove myself academically.

My lack of qualifications hadn't been an issue while I was an army officer, but as I advanced through the police force, it kept cropping up again and again. Every time I was interviewed for a promotion, they queried why it was that I'd never got any more qualifications, nor been to university. For the top brass, I think it always left a bit of a question mark over my name.

Nevertheless, after having run police stations at Stoke Newington and later at Hampstead, I moved into a central HR job at Scotland Yard, where I was responsible for running management development strategy for the Met. I'd long held a fascination for leadership and here I was starting to get into the nuts and bolts of it – and I loved it.

As part of the role, I would organise MBA opportunities for some of our high-potential officers and, at some point, this took me on a research trip down to Exeter University. There, I met Alan Hooper, a former Royal Marine about my age, and head of the leadership programme. I got on well with Alan and not long after I'd got back to London, I found an excuse to ring him up and enquire about MPhil degrees at the university.

He explained that an MPhil was a Master's degree but wasn't taught, so you could do a particular piece of research, subject to your capability, and you'd then produce a paper that could eventually develop into a PhD.

"Who have you got in mind for it?" he asked.

When I explained it would be for me, that I was looking for a challenge, he was quite taken aback.

"You're a senior guy in the police, John, what on earth do you need challenge for?"

Unperturbed, I pressed him on what would be required for someone to get onto the course.

"You'd just need to apply and I'm sure we'd find you acceptable, providing you've got a good first degree," he said.

I went a quiet at the other end of the line. "I don't actually have a first degree," I said.

"Really? I've got to say I'm really surprised you haven't got a degree. OK, what are your A levels like?"

I started to feel awkward, "Well, I left school early, so I don't have any of those either."

At this, he started to chuckle. Whether it was with awe or disbelief that I'd made it this far without either of these qualifications, I wasn't sure, but he started to explain that there was another way in. If I could submit examples of papers or strategic documents that I'd written, then these could count towards demonstrating my eligibility for a place on the course. Fortunately, these I had, both from my time in the force and from that brief stint at Wolfson College in Cambridge when I'd had my epiphany about rowing.

— • —

In 1992, I started a MPhil in leadership and organisational behaviour at Exeter. That year, I set myself the goal of doing the two hardest things that I could imagine doing, two things that I had never really done before: tackling something academic and working alone on a project. These were two things that, up until this point, I had felt were almost impossible.

I treated it like climbing a mountain: I just settled in and did it. One hold at a time, gradually making my way up the rock face. The Met had kindly agreed to give me a part-time sabbatical, so I was able to have a hell of a lot of time off to concentrate on my research. This I was grateful for because, although the research would have some bearing on the management development that I was doing at the Met at the time, this was, ultimately, a personal endeavour – an old ghost that I needed to lay to rest.

People say love is wasted on the young, but I guess that the same might be said for education. When you approach education at a later age, you really have chosen it and I gave the course 120 per cent every moment I was on it.

I was 49 years old when I went up to collect my MPhil. I can honestly say it was one of the happiest days of my life. It had demanded of me things that no other expedition or adventure ever had, but it felt like a wall had come down and that I could finally step through and move on.

— • —

As it would happen, my interest and obsessions with leadership, adventure and wild places, would finally start to coalesce with my qualification from Exeter.

My old climbing partner, Alan Caudell, whose farmhouse Derwent Folds had been our base in the Lake District, told me he was going to have to sell the house. His fortunes were running dry in the recession and he could no longer afford to pay the mortgage. Heartbroken at the thought of losing the place that had given us so much over the years, I promised that if I could find some business opportunities that I would rent the place off him.

Back in London, I talked to some friends and we managed to get a small business going that would provide leadership and development courses for companies. We based it at the farmhouse and called it Derwent Management Development. It was part-time, as I was still in the police, but soon took off enough for the revenue to more than cover Alan's mortgage.

The more courses that I ran, the more I felt that there was simply a certain magic about the place that was hard to replicate anywhere else. Some locations have a real energising and almost spiritual aura around them, which makes good work come so much more naturally, and Derwent Folds was one of them. Every time that I drove away from there, I felt alive, ready to take on anything that life could throw at me.

Alan Caudell's old farmhouse, Derwent Folds, in the Lake District, and the site of much of my development work with teams over the years.

THIRTEEN
The Boss

B y 1993, I'd been appointed to the National Police Staff College in Hampshire to help run intensive, three-month programmes for senior police officers who were preparing to command a police division. It was quite a challenge to have a room full of seasoned and, in some cases, hardened senior police officers – many of whom were a lot older and more operationally experienced than myself. Some would be only too willing to give me a good run for my money until you could find some common ground and get them on side.

One summer Friday afternoon, I was preparing next week's lectures in the old mansion block that formed the police college library in Hampshire when one of the academic staff approached me. I remembered him as running the special course, an accelerated promotion course for young high-fliers. Each year, 20 or 30 young officers would be selected for fast-track development and expected to go on to become future leaders of the police service.

I'd always been envious of this lecturer, because the special course was one that I would have loved to run. He told me that he had a new group of students coming in on Monday at four o'clock and was in a bit of a dilemma: he had no senior police officer to give them an introductory address. Could I do it?

My first thought was to put him off as I had a fresh group of students arriving myself that day, but he insisted that no one else was available. I reluctantly agreed, knowing that now half of my weekend would be taken up preparing the damn speech. It was to be only 10 minutes long but as Winston Churchill said, "If I have to make a two-hour speech, I can prepare it in ten minutes; if it's a ten minute speech, it can take me two hours."

I thought about the speech on the long-drive back to Essex. I decided that if these were to be young leaders of the future, then I should really try to fire them up. I'd base my speech on Ernest Shackleton, who'd long been a hero of mine.

When four o'clock on Monday came round, I made my way to the auditorium to deliver my speech to the 20 or so incoming bright young things. As I walked down the corridor, in full uniform, I noticed that herds of other police officers were making their way into the room. The lecturer who'd commissioned me to do the speech was on the door.

"Hello John, I was worried you weren't going to come," he said, obviously relieved to see me.

"Why are all these people streaming into the auditorium?" I asked.

He looked at me blankly: "What do you mean?" I told him that I was expecting 20 high-fliers, where upon it dawned on him the mistake that I'd made.

"Sorry John, I'm not running the special course anymore – this is the junior command course for inspectors and chief inspectors."

I looked at him in horror. "I can't possibly deliver this speech to that group," I uttered. "These are all mature police officers, it's going to be completely inappropriate!"

He didn't seem to see what all the fuss was about; besides, he said, I had no choice now, we'd run out of time and were about to start.

With that, he marched down the long carpet to the front of the auditorium and announced to the audience how lucky they were to have such a distinguished leader to give the opening address, and would they please welcome Chief Superintendent John Peck to the stage.

"Oh sod it," I thought, "I can't change it now," and walked into the room.

I stood for a while at the front of the stage looking out at the hardened faces staring back at me.

"It's a good time for young people to be here," I started. "There's much to be done. Never before has the British Police Force been in such a state of disarray. All around you, I see senior police officers, impotent, unable to find a way to lead us into the future."

There was a sharp intake of breath from the floor.

I kept going, eulogising about Shackleton as an example of how to lead your men when everyone's at their lowest ebb. Even when he asked them to do the most uncomfortable things, they would do it for "The Boss", as they called him.

I told the story of a day in his Trans-Antarctica expedition of 1914–17 when the crew of the *Endurance* had been desperately rowing their boats for two days in an effort to reach a safer haven at Elephant Island. Shackleton had stood up on a mound of snow and ice to take a sighting with his sextant and caught a brief glimpse of the sun, only to find that they had drifted back many miles and had made no progress. He had never felt more lonely in that moment, but had found it within himself to urge them on, to tell them they were doing alright and making good progress.

To my complete surprise, the audience seemed to be on the edge of their seats.

"You see, Shackleton really loved those men," I continued. "My tip for you, if you want to lead your men like Shackleton did, is simple: just love them from the bottom of your heart and they will follow you to the ends of the earth."

There was a stunned silence. With that, I picked up my papers and walked with my head up out of the room. As I passed the group of instructors at the back of the room, they looked down and avoided eye contact. It seemed to continue the next day; as I walked about the corridors of the college, the officers that had attended the lecture looked at me in a strange, uneasy way.

Two days later, I was having dinner in the dining hall with some of the other lecturers when one of them leaned over to me.

"I've got to say, John, that talk was just amazing. I've never heard one talk generate so much debate. People can't stop talking about it – they're saying they've never heard a senior police officer talk like that."

A few of the others nodded in agreement.

"What about you, Jack?" I asked the grizzled old inspector sitting next to me, "What did you think about it?"

He slowly put down his knife and fork.

"To be honest, when you started I thought you'd lost your marbles and that the guys would never follow you. And then I felt you had them absolutely gripped. Only at the very end did you lose them, when you mentioned the 'L' word – then you must have lost them completely."

We all broke out into fits of laughter. How extraordinary I thought, that all those police officers could face deranged criminals, terrorist bombers, dead bodies – the lot – but the word "love" really freaked them out.

— • —

Inspirational leadership is hard to define and yet we know it when we see it. I can picture people in my mind now who I've worked with in the past and fit that bill. Everyone can be a good manager. Most people can be taught to be an effective leader. But truly inspirational leaders, like Shackleton, are a rare breed and a joy to work with – and that has something to do with character, I think.

Over the years, the business of charismatic leadership has risen and waned, and is now unfashionable. People feel slightly uncomfortable about it because it can be seen as a bit narcissistic – all about personality, not process – and, in its own way, alienating. The pressure to be charismatic can be threatening to people who don't think they are.

But the reality is, if you're trying to deliver change, if you're trying to take people to where they don't think they can go, the only way to do it is to inspire them, and to do that, you need to use charismatic skills. They've got to believe in you and, most of the time, that comes down to the simplest things.

What I took from being an army officer was that my responsibility for my men and their welfare was as important as achieving the so-called important objectives that I was set. In fact, one couldn't be separated from the other. Some people in my platoon couldn't read or write, so I used to write their letters home for them. I was only 19, but I felt like a father figure to them and we had a close bond that made them feel like my own sons. Very often, we'd be away for 20 days at a time in the jungle or up country, and it was up to me keep them fired up and make them feel a bit special.

When we'd come back in from an exercise, my platoon would shower, eat their food, then clean and inspect their weapons and kit. Then, I'd have to go into the barrack room and inspect all their kit. It was implicitly understood that I would not have a shower until every one of those guys had finished. They could then head off and have fun, and I would have to go and clean my own stuff up. God help you, if you went back early yourself.

It was the same in the field – I'd eat my food after everyone else got theirs. It was absolutely unthinkable that I'd be seen eating anything until every one of my soldiers had been fed. As officers, if we were taking them on a run, we ran at the front with them. We took all the same shitty risks that they did. They'd respect us for that and wouldn't mind if we lived in an "officer's mess".

I have some happy memories of that time. I always thought then, as I do now, that my main responsibility was to keep up the morale of my men.

— • —

I spent the next 18 months running leadership programmes at the police college and loved the work. But as I was away from home five nights a week and then travelling back and forth between Essex and Hampshire on a very fast motorbike, which my wife was convinced would end in tears, the separation was taking a toll on my marriage. It was time to move on.

I had discovered there was a clause in my pension whereby I could leave the police force at 50, having completed 26 years of service. I decided to take it. Derwent Management Development, the team development business I was running outside of the police, was flourishing and Elaine and I decided that we would have a crack at running it full-time.

I had a small retirement get-together with my fellow lecturers at the police college. While I was making my farewell speech, I remember a loud cracking noise. As I looked out through the tall windows of the old mansion block across the grounds, I saw this huge, old oak tree crack and slowly fall to the ground, its branches splintering in all directions. I took the falling tree as a sign – the closing of a chapter in the book and the start of a new life outside the police.

As a Chief Superintendent in the Metropolitan Police.

FOURTEEN
Keep Your Head

The door to my office at home was always open. This was largely because its contents seemed desperate to escape around the house – whether it was piles of books, files or bits of kit – blocking the door and creating a haphazard space that gave the impression, at least, of being a hive of activity.

One Saturday, my youngest son Julian wandered in. He'd not long turned 18 and, as he would be leaving school that summer, asked me if I could help him arrange an expedition for him and few of his friends once their exams were out of the way. They had their heart set on a jungle trek. I told him to leave it with me for a few days while I called Richard Shuff.

Richard Shuff, or "Shuffy" as I now affectionately called him, had spent much of his early life in some very taxing roles in the military, where he'd spend weeks at a time alone tracking insurgents in the Malaysian jungle. But as soon as he got out of the army, he'd resolved to put something back into life and had set up West Coast Adventures for young disadvantaged kids from Glasgow's Gorbals.

He and I had become good friends after I had contacted him in

1988 about running one of his wilderness programmes for inner-city kids from Hackney. My two oldest sons had also both been on his course out on the Scottish island of Luing in their mid-teens and I saw staggering changes take place over the time that they were with him.

I remember Elaine and I arriving at Victoria Coach Station to pick them up after a week in Luing. We couldn't see them at first, until we realised that the young men walking towards us were our sons. Twenty years on, they still recount tales from that week – of having spent it living in a cave, surviving on seaweed and prising limpets out of rock pools. I wanted Julian and his mates to have a similarly raw experience. Shuffy didn't disappoint.

— • —

That summer, Julian and six of his good mates from school – all now free of their studies – his brother Chris, Shuffy and I found ourselves in the Malaysian state of Pahang. We were in a town called Jerantut, on the edge of Taman Negara National Park – the largest untouched rainforest left on the peninsula. Shuffy, who knew the area as a former outpost of the British Army, had flown out a week earlier to arrange our guides and the boats that would get us to our forward base in the remote village of Kampung Buntal.

We had just a day to acclimatise and gather the remaining supplies. Since the local shops offered very little choice of non-perishable food, other than tins of sardines, it looked like our staple diet was going to be fairly one-dimensional. We bought as many tins as we could find.

The next day we set off for Buntal, some 60 miles into the jungle and reachable only via the River Tembeling. We made it in a single push, but, from here, we would start to enter the interior proper. We swapped into smaller boats to continue our journey up the Tembeling to Kuala Lukut, which is just about the end of the navigable water, and then continued on foot for a couple more hours until we reached our first camp.

We would be spending the first night with a family of native Orang Asli of the Batek people. One of the Asli had given birth just three days before we arrived, and we were awestruck by the ease with which she – and the other Asli – generously lit fires and constructed shelters for us to spend the night in.

We relished the generous hospitality of our hosts. Nights in the tropical jungle can be as warm and humid as the days and, for the next five days, we would be sleeping in hammocks slung between trees, under a mosquito net, sticky with sweat that turned cold as the temperature finally dipped just before sunrise.

— • —

A small hurricane had passed through this area not long before we'd arrived and, as we set off the next morning, we quickly encountered the havoc that it had wreaked on the forest. It had left fallen trees like pick-up-sticks in its wake, slowing our progress as we were continually forced to clamber up and over them. This made navigation difficult, even for our local guide, Din, who had spent much of his life as a hunter.

Richard Shuff leads some of my son Julian's friends
through the Malaysian jungle in 2001.

We pressed on for several days, often following a river bed and occasionally breaking off to cut out a meander in its course, as we went deeper into the jungle.

On the third day, we ascended to 2,600 feet and crossed into the state of Kelantan – before making a long and dangerous descent as the light faded. I had been walking behind Din and could tell he was anxious; he was struggling to find his way with so many landmarks missing, felled or swept away by the hurricane.

We eventually came across a disused camp ground, which Din said had probably been used by another group of Orang Asli. Since dusk wasn't far off, he suggested that we make camp for the night here. The team found spots to string up their hammocks and bivouac sheets among the trees and they settled in to cook their food, while Richard and I made camp further along the clearing.

— • —

The jungle is wholly different from any other wilderness environment that I have spent time in. The phenomenal noise from the orchestra of monkeys, frog and insects at dawn and dusk overruns your senses, tapping into some deep recess in your mind long since forgotten. The extreme humidity makes it feel as if everything is closing in, while the insects constantly circle or crawl all over you and drive you mad. The volume of snakes is such that you could easily step on one if the local guides do not see them first. And, of course, there is the fear of getting lost in a wilderness where doing so could be so easy.

Darkness was settling over the forest when the guide's younger brother approached us. It was his job to stay at the back of the group and backslash the trees with his machete to mark our route in case we needed to return the same way. He was very shy and had resisted any attempt that Richard had made in the past to make conversation with him, so we were surprised to find him now standing nearby, desperate to talk.

"*Din pergi, Din pergi, tidak faham di sini Din pergi*," he kept saying, each time repeating it more loudly in the hope that it would help us understand. Fortunately, Richard did understand, translating it roughly as: "*Din gone, Din gone, don't know where Din go*". We had assumed that Din had gone fishing, having seen him netting fish earlier in the day, but the boy said that he couldn't have as the nets were still here at camp. Perhaps he had gone hunting? No, the boy explained, he would never have left without his torch, which was still here.

Shuffy started to wonder if Din had got lost.

"The local guides never use maps," he said, but judging by his British military OS sheet, we had veered too far north west.

"We certainly shouldn't have encountered 2,000 feet of steep descent."

He might have just gone off to check things out, I suggested, but Shuffy said that would be unlikely because guides didn't like travelling after dark in the forest for fear of treading on snakes.

Din's brother kept plucking at his throat, suggesting that his brother was lying injured somewhere. By now, it was dark and while I didn't like the idea of something having happened to the guide, we still had six teenagers that we needed to get out of the jungle.

"Ask him if he could find his way out of the jungle if his brother did not return," I said to Shuffy.

The boy raised his shoulders in a shrug; he looked dubious. He was desperate to search for his brother, but we persuaded him that it was too dangerous – telling him to hold fire until morning and that he was welcome to have something to eat with us. He couldn't eat, not until he knew that his brother was safe, he said, and walked to the edge of the clearing to set up his basha shelter alone.

I turned to Richard, who looked grave – we were in serious trouble without a guide. I started rummaging in my rucksack.

"What are you looking for?" he asked.

"Something that might help us."

I think Richard thought I had a GPS, but instead I pulled out a bottle of Rusty Nail – a mixture of whisky and Southern Comfort. He laughed; but we both took a swig to steady the nerves.

Julian came over to see what was going on. He had been watching us from a distance and sussed we might be in trouble. I decided to explain the situation to him.

"Do you want me to tell anyone else?" he asked.

Keep it to himself for now, I told him, explaining that we weren't going to keep people in the dark, but that Richard and I needed some time to get a plan together. He agreed and as he walked back to join his friends, I felt proud at how he'd handled himself – it would've been just as easy for a young guy of his age to lose his head.

— • —

I had taken an old book into the jungle written by a guy called Geert Hofstede. He was a former IBM employee and had conducted a study into differences in international business culture. I had been reading it the night before and I'd been interested by something Hofstede had called "uncertainty avoidance", which seemed pertinent now.

For Hofstede, uncertainty left unchecked led to anxiety, which didn't help anybody because it had no real object. Fear, on the other hand, was based on a real risk and that you could plan for. So, to me, that suggested that, if you were in a flat in London and were lying in bed worried that a tiger would come in and attack you – what you were feeling was anxiety. But if you were in the Malaysian jungle, where you had seen tiger footprints during the day and were now lying in your hammock at night worrying about the tiger, then you had a right to feel fear.

I was explaining all this to Shuffy as we sat drinking our Rusty Nail. What we needed to do, I said, was to turn our uncertainty into a risk – that way we could do some scenario planning and work how to manage it. I don't know exactly what he made of it, but he gave me the benefit of the doubt.

We both agreed that there was nothing practical that we could do until the next morning. At daybreak, we could conduct an organised search in the immediate vicinity of the camp – I was used to doing searches in the police, albeit not in thick jungle. There was a good chance that Din would turn up by then with any luck, we thought; but, if he didn't, then he was clearly lost or worse, dead, and we would have to move to Plan B.

I asked Richard how long we could survive in the jungle with the limited food supplies that we had with us. His answer was more optimistic than I expected.

"The river water is safe enough to drink and people could last for 10 days at least, living off certain plants and catching fish with the nets that the guides had left behind. Eventually, after 10 days, I would hope we could find our way to safety."

I was just thinking that the situation wasn't as dire as I expected, when we heard a rustling from the bushes nearby and our guide miraculously appeared, safe and sound.

Despite what we'd thought, he had left camp to do a reconnaissance to reassure himself that even though we might have been slightly off-route, we were not, in fact, lost.

He had followed a stream that had led circuitously back past the previous night's camp and would eventually take us to the camp that we had shared with the Asli. His brother had been nervous simply because he had never before been on his own with a group of Europeans and, of course, Din had not announced his departure to either him or ourselves.

Richard and I laugh about the incident now, but when Din showed up that night, I had never been so relieved to see anyone in my life.

— • —

True to Din's promise, the following morning, we picked up the tributary of the Sungai Lurut and were delighted, after another day and night in the jungle, to make it back to where the Asli were camped. Din had made a deal with them before we left and, in our absence, they had made us some very fine bamboo rafts with tillers of split bamboo and even luggage platforms and seats.

We set off for Kuala Lukut, paddling and poling away on our elaborate rafts. At midday, we passed a group of Asli who were boiling up jungle fruit to sell downriver. We had planned to camp there but we were making good progress, so Shuffy convinced us to push on and make Buntal in a single day to avoid the rather imposing thunderstorm that had been chasing downstream.

We made Buntal, exhausted, just as night was closing in and the first rain drops were sounding against the canopy.

FIFTEEN

Turn Right When The Butter Starts To Melt

I was working in the Lakes when Elaine called late to tell me about a couple that she had just seen interviewed on television. A woman called Debra Searle and her husband had entered a race to row across the Atlantic, but several days into the race the husband had found that he couldn't continue. They had both decided to abandon the race and called for a rescue, but, when the support vessel finally arrived, Debra decided that she would stay on the boat and continue rowing alone. She succeeded, arriving in Barbados weeks later to much acclaim.

I was absolutely fascinated by the story. How, I wondered, does anyone – let alone two ordinary people – decide to get into a rowing boat on the Canary Islands and row themselves more than three thousand miles to Barbados? And yet, Debra had done it. Maybe lots more people had.

When I arrived home to Essex a week or so later, the idea was still nagging at me. I searched the internet for "rowing the Atlantic" and came up with a website for a couple of guys who had made a successful crossing. I couldn't resist giving the number on the site a call.

Rowing across the Atlantic was not an impossible prospect, they assured me – far from it. I asked if I needed to be an experienced rower: the answer was no. Would I need to be familiar navigating big seas? They said all this could be learnt. What about getting hold of a boat? They pointed me to a website where people advertise second-hand rowing boats for hire or sale. I checked and, sure enough, there were several boats available.

By the time that I got off the phone, I was so caught up in the enthusiasm of the rower that I'd spoken to that I immediately started ringing round the adverts. I wasn't *really* going to row across the Atlantic, I just wanted to *see* if there was, by any chance, a boat still available.

The first person that I called told me that the boat had been taken just the day before. But the second boat was still available. It belonged to John Searson, an experienced ocean rower who had endured a similar trial to Debra Searle: his partner had had to be airlifted from the boat, while he had carried on to finish the race alone. We talked for a while and I told him that I was keen on the boat, but I needed to figure out how I was going to get the money to rent it from him. I said I would call back.

— • —

By that evening, I had made some enquiries and there was a vague suggestion that I might get some sponsorship for the project. This initial flush of hope was all that I needed. The next day I telephoned John Searson and promptly sent off a cheque for £1,000 as deposit on his ocean rowing boat. *Now* I was hooked.

I had no concept at this stage that that £1,000 would turn out to be just the first of about 27 similar-sized cheques that I would I send out to all manner of suppliers to get this project off the ground. Perhaps if I had known this – or the 18 months of hell that I would drag my family and colleagues through – I would never have had the courage to move forward.

But this state of innocence is as inevitable as it is necessary for any project of this nature. The writer Carol Pearson, whose book, *The Hero Within*, charts this early stage of a journey, once told me that if anyone seriously considered the reality of starting their own business in full knowledge of the difficulties that they were going to face, the majority would never set out on that journey.

For me, I can only describe wanting to rowing across the Atlantic as like a love affair – I was intoxicated with the idea of it and I couldn't pull back until it was done. I had a boat; now I needed a partner.

— • —

One of the people who responded to my advert in the police newspaper for the Himalayan climbing expedition in 1986 was a guy called Fraser Dodds. At that time, Fraser had been his early 30s; he was well over six foot and fighting fit. He was an operational police sergeant and I imagined that he was a popular and effective leader, given how he bounced into my office that morning.

Before joining the police he had been in the army for several years as an infantryman and had clearly loved his time there. When I asked him what he had done in the past to qualify him to come climbing in the Himalayas, he told me that he played second row for Watford Rugby Club firsts.

I remember laughing to myself wondering what on earth that had to do with climbing mountains, but his enthusiastic delivery somehow convinced me that it did. I asked him how he was going to raise the money to fund his share of the expedition costs and he said simply, "I'll sell my flat."

I invited Fraser to the selection event in Alps and he proved to be an instant success. When I told him I that I wanted him on the team, he was chuffed. He put his flat on the market the next day and sold it, only to win several thousand pounds on the pools a few weeks later – which would have been more than enough to cover the expedition.

He had struggled with bad altitude sickness on the climb of Jogin I, but had refused to let it stop him reaching the top. It was a miracle that he got back down to safety, as we would later find at base camp that he was in the early stages of suffering pulmonary oedema.

In 1991, he had proved a natural rower and enormously good fun on our record-breaking row across the Channel. Now, as I sat pondering who would make a good partner for the Atlantic rowing expedition, I wondered if Fraser might be the man.

The first thing that a lot of previous ocean rowers had told me was that I needed to think seriously about whether it might be better to row solo. In fact, one rower that I spoke to had wholeheartedly advised against rowing it as a pair. It wasn't the sharks or the 30-foot waves that were most likely to kill you when crossing the Atlantic, he'd said, it was the other guy in the boat.

I thought about the many adventurers that I had come across in the past and tried to imagine spending 12 weeks in small rowing boat with them. One by one, they dropped off my list – not least because I knew that many of them wouldn't entertain the idea of going with me either – until, at last, I narrowed it down to Fraser Dodds.

I wondered what would be the best way to approach him about it and, in the end, simply suggested that we meet for a pint in a London pub to talk about "a possible future adventure". By the time that we met, Fraser was thoroughly intrigued. I told him about the Atlantic Ocean race and my plan to do it next year, and then I asked him if he would come with me.

He jumped out of his seat, threw his arms around me in a giant bear hug and said, "I'm your man John, let's do it!"

We sank a few pints of Guinness to seal the deal and I left the pub in great spirits: I had a team for this remarkable adventure.

— • —

Early one morning about three weeks later, I received a call from Fraser. He sounded stressed, almost in tears at the other end of the line. "John, I can't do it. I'm so sorry to let you down but I'm not going to be able to row across the Atlantic with you."

Unlike me, he was still in the police force and explained that he had just come to the end of a very exacting and dangerous role in SO19 – the crack firearms unit that deal only with arresting armed criminals. He'd been with the unit for 18 months and had had some pretty hair-raising experiences.

Now, he had promised his wife Bernadette that he would settle down, concentrate on passing his promotion exam to become an inspector and spend more time with their young son Ruari.

I could tell that Fraser had made up his mind, that he had to take the pressure off for both him and Bernadette for a bit. I told him not to worry, that it was understandable – which, of course it was – and checked that he was still on for the sea canoeing trip in Scotland that we had planned for a couple of months time. He said that he was, and we left it at that.

When I came off the phone, Elaine could see that I was devastated by the news. I felt like the bottom had fallen out of my world. Together, we tried to think of other people that we could approach.

"There is one person who I know would be great," I said, playing it over in my mind.

"Who?" she asked.

"Julian!"

Julian is our youngest son and he and I have always got on incredibly well. But my suggestion didn't go down well.

"You are not taking him on that boat. It's bad enough the thought of you getting killed out there, without you taking one of our sons with you!"

I couldn't argue with that and said that if all else failed, I would go alone.

— • —

Three months later, Fraser and I met up on the west coast of Scotland as planned. Nothing had been mentioned about the ocean crossing and we were having a great time canoeing from one remote island to another.

On the second night, we had got a small campfire going and were sitting round it, chewing over the day with a bottle of scotch, when Fraser asked if I'd found a new crew member yet. I told him that I hadn't and that I might do it alone.

"Christ, you can't do that John!" he said.

There was a moment's silence and then he put one hand on my shoulder and said: "Oh fuck it! I'll come with you."

I tried to put him off; said he must think about Bernadette first, but, this time, he told me not to worry.

"She'll let me go, I think she's probably fed up of me hanging around looking miserable anyway."

My heart warmed to him and I felt a huge weight lift off my shoulders. I knew Elaine and the boys would be relieved, too. They had warned me against the prospect of going alone, knowing that being a bit of an extrovert, I would need the strength of another person to bolster me when times got hard.

As soon as we got back from the trip, we started planning in earnest. While I worked on preparing our boat, Fraser dealt with the logistics. The race was being organised by the Ocean Rowing Society and, having had our application for the race accepted, we were soon invited to one of their dinners.

The society was presided over by Kenneth Crutchlow – a man who would become our key mentor on the row. There were nearly 100 ocean rowers (or ORs as they called each other) and their wives and husbands. The atmosphere was electric and I cannot remember spending an evening with a more interesting group of people. Many had already crossed the Atlantic successfully; others, like us, were going to be taking part in the race in January and were in the process of planning their trip.

Fraser brought Bernadette along to the dinner and, despite the fervour of the evening, Elaine and I were left wondering whether she really believed that Frazer was going to go through with this madcap idea.

— • —

Bernadette is one of the nicest people I have ever met. I have an enduring memory of her sitting on Fraser's knee in a miniskirt in a Covent Garden cafe after celebrating our successful return from the Himalayas. We had all been drinking a lot of champagne as we had just been told that our expedition sponsor was going to give every team member back the money that they had put in. You can imagine how happy we were.

Bernadette turned and whispered something into Fraser's ear.

"What did you say?" he said.

At the top of her voice she shouted: "I said, 'I love you Fraser!'"

He was stricken with embarrassment and was trying to shut her up, but she just kept shouting, "I love you Fraser!" louder and louder, much to the hysterics of all his friends.

Many months after our dinner with the Ocean Rowing Society, Bernadette would come home from work to find Fraser and Ruari sitting on the floor of their living room surrounded by bags of groceries.

"What's going on here?" she asked.

"Ruari and I are just packing stuff up for my Atlantic trip."

She told Elaine later that this was the first time that she realised Fraser was serious – though it wasn't until she heard we were out to sea that she really believed it would happen.

— • —

With the date of the race soon upon us, Fraser, Elaine and I found ourselves renting a flat on the little island of La Gomera near Tenerife, frantically packing and repacking our supplies into the our ocean rowing boat *New Horizons*, which was now being offloaded onto shore, ready to be craned into the harbour.

Fraser had dreaded that it would be too emotional for him to have Bernadette and Ruari at the start line, so had asked that they both just flew out to meet him at the other end in the Barbados.

As we assembled our gear, we were surrounded by a dozen or so other boat crews and we did all that we could to support and encourage each other. While, technically, we were competitors in a race, there was only one serious enemy and we all shared it: the weather and wild seas of the Atlantic Ocean.

Elaine had been convinced, from the start, that this ocean row would end in death. It was only when she saw the other 10 or so rowing boats like ours, and started speaking with some of those had succeeded in the past, that she began to actually believe it might be possible for us to survive the ordeal.

— • —

An hour before we set off, the owner of our boat, John Searson, who had flown out with us to the start line, was helping us remove any unnecessary junk from the cubby holes. He picked up my sextant.

"What are you taking this for?" he said.

I told him that I'd been on an ocean yachtmaster course to learn how to take sightings from the sun and the stars (not that I had a tremendous amount of confidence in my ability to do so at that point).

He told me that, having done this row himself, taking sightings from a lurching boat in the middle of the Atlantic was more than a little tricky and that we'd be better off with a simple GPS.

I was heartily relieved not to be having to deal with the stress of having to use the complicated set of logarithmic charts that came with the sextant, and promptly offloaded them as well. I dug out a handheld GPS from my kit and, with about 20 minutes to go until we were due on the start line, I tried to start it up. I was sure that Fraser would know how to use it, but he was equally mystified.

Starting to panic, I asked around among the guys who were now freeing off the boats so that they could start edging out to the start line. Reluctantly, a nearby skipper offered to see if he could set it up. The minutes were ticking by. Much longer and we were going to have edge out to the start line ourselves. The skipper chucked me the GPs at the last moment.

"Should work OK," he said.

As the start gun sounded and we pulled away next to the other boats, Fraser and I looked at each other, wondering how the hell we were going to navigate with this thing.

"Let's just follow everyone else," I said, reading his thoughts.

So, for a while, we did – until the waves got bigger and it got darker, and we found ourselves alone at sea with a GPS that we couldn't use and 3,000 miles of Atlantic Ocean to cross. Well, this really was turning into an adventure.

— • —

In describing his ascent of Everest, Bear Grylls, then the youngest climber to have done so, recalls some advice that his mother gave him before he left. She reminded him that commitment is "doing what you said you would do long after the feeling that you had when saying it has passed". I held this sentiment close to my own heart as Fraser and I pushed off the jetty at La Gomera and headed for Barbados.

It seems ridiculous now that we could not have realised at the time what an awesome undertaking such a task would be. But until we set off on 20th January 2004, we had no concept of the storms that we would be rowing in and, indeed, the fear that a 30-foot wave can instil in you as it barrels up behind your tiny boat. Out there, you literally are but a drop in the ocean. The scale of the challenge comes upon you quickly.

As soon as the second day, you realise there is no turning back; rather, you realise that the only thing you can do is to keep the boat moving as fast as you can in order to get the ordeal over as quickly as you can.

This is achievable if you stick to your routine: two hours on, two hours off. Continuously. Day and night. Until you hit land 3,000 miles away. Imagine going to your local gym, sitting on the rowing machine and rowing for two hours. Then imagine doing this every two hours for nine weeks. This was the reality of the commitment that we had made.

— • —

For many months before an event, Elaine will tell me that, in my mind, I have already left on the expedition. I wake at four o'clock in the morning, tossing and turning, imaging all sorts of scenarios that could happen and how I am going to deal with them.

Running up to the row, there was one dilemma that haunted me more than any other. It was the thought that, in a high storm, the boat's rudder would break or jam and that the wire cable leading to the tiller would be stuck in one position, rendering the boat liable to turn into the wind, be caught broadside on and thrown over, upside down.

Each night, I would turn this problem over in my mind. During the day, I would practise ways of solving it: detaching the wire from the rudder and replacing it with a mechanism that you'd find on a sailing dinghy, where you steer via a couple of thin lines running through cleats on the side of the boat.

My rowing partner, Fraser Dodds, taking his turn at the oars.

This is how it went for a couple of months, such was the extent of my fear that this could happen.

Then, three days out into the Atlantic… it did. Hit by our first storm, and in an effort to steady the boat, we threw out our sea anchor. This is, essentially, a giant parachute that trails on a line behind the boat, stopping it from turning parallel onto the incoming waves. At some stage during this process, the trailing rope had snagged on the rudder and bent the wire leading to our steering controls. It was dark and, with sunken hearts, we realised that we wouldn't be able to row effectively with the rudder jammed.

The covered part of our boat had a little hatch at the back that sat almost directly above the rudder. I resolved that as soon as there was enough daylight, I would crawl inside, climb out of the hatch and reach down under the water and detach the wire.

We waited out the night. Fraser was, by now, understandably anxious about the danger associated with this move, as the waves coming behind us were now 20 to 30-foot and building. They could come crashing down on the back of the boat at any point. But I insisted that this was the only way to continue our adventure.

I got the spanner and screwdriver that I had prepared for just this moment, opened the tiny hatch and squeezed the top half of my body through. Fraser hung onto my legs to stop me getting sucked out and I reached down and undid the vital piece – knowing that if I dropped it into the sea, we would be virtually unable to keep the boat straight for the rest of the trip.

The whole operation took about two and half minutes and, as I released the wire, I realised that the back of the boat, where I was kneeling, was at sea level. Our little boat would go up a wave and keep going up like in a lift, get to the top, then teeter, giving me a view that seemed endless and then, down, down, down the other side we'd go to where another wave would be waiting for us.

It reminded me so much of when we had been caught in that storm in the Channel in 1975, when I first understood the power of waves like this – and here I was, once again, trying to keep the damn boat going in a straight line!

I slithered back down through the hatch to the cabin below and slammed the hatch shut. Within a moment of flipping its locks, I felt the tremendous crashing of a wave on the back of the boat. We had been spared again.

But having made sure that we would be able to turn the boat, we now needed to know when to turn. Our route was to go down south along the African coast until we came to some islands called Cape Verde. At this point, we were to simply "turn right" and head west to Barbados.

Before we had left, I had asked an seasoned yachtsman, who was used to sailing the trade winds, about how we would know when to make the turn.

"Just turn right when the butter starts to melt," he'd said.

We, of course, didn't have any butter on board with us. With all our dehydrated food to save space, there was no room for luxuries such as butter. Fortunately, John Searson, from whom we'd hired the boat, had rowed this route before and, from time to time, we were able to reach him on our satellite phone. We explained where we were and his advice was simply "just keep going south".

Buoyed by his assurances, we rowed on with enthusiasm and were making great speed to Cape Verde. But within a few days, our satellite link was telling us that some of our competitors were starting to swing right. "That's too early, isn't it?" we thought. It was becoming abundantly clear that neither Fraser nor I had a clear idea of the protocols around making this decision. We just had this vague notion that somehow the wind would start veering west when the time was right – after all, that's what trade winds did wasn't it? We decided just to keep ploughing on south.

Two days later, we were a hundred miles south of Cape Verde and were starting to get nervous. I put a call through to Searson.

"What the hell are you guys doing down there? You should have turned west two days ago!" he yelled. "You've gone far too far south. Christ, John, you're going to have a hell of a job getting up to Barbados from there."

Our worst nightmare was already coming true. I put the phone down and climbed out of the cabin to tell Fraser about our predicament. He looked despairingly at me, knowing that his family would be waiting for him in Barbados.

"What's going to happen John?"

I hesitated for a moment. "Well, this far south, we'll probably end up in Venezuela," I said.

"But we don't even have any charts of the Venezuelan coastline!" he replied.

"Well, it's pretty big so eventually we're bound to bump into it," I said.

"Exactly – bump into it. More likely smash into the rocks."

This was not how it was supposed to go. I had worked hard for a year before we left studying sextant readings, and had even passed the Royal Yachting Association's exam on ocean navigation. Fraser had passed a similar exam dealing with the practicalities of sailing a boat of the kind that now seemed destined to carry us to South America.

I had even spoken to John Searson, who himself was a meteorologist, for guidance on weather patterns. Why had I never had a serious conversation with him about this crucial part of the route? It would have been the simplest thing in the world for me to have said to him: "John, when we get to the point of Cape Verde, will you stay on duty and simply tell us when to turn west?"

He would have known by then that our minds might already be dulled enough by the days at sea not to have made a sensible decision. Instead, he had gone off duty for the weekend and assumed that we knew what we were doing.

I tried to cheer Fraser up with a vision of white sandy beaches, girls with grass skirts and piña coladas that might await us in Venezuela, but he didn't seem convinced.

"Seriously John, what are we going to do?"

I told him not to worry, that I would call Elaine and that she was good at finding ways out of situations like this. I picked up the satellite phone and dialled home.

I described our predicament to Elaine: that we desperately needed to get a feel for what the current pattern was south of Cape Verde and asked her if she could so some research. She protested that she knew nothing about boats or currents but when I explained that our lives were at stake, she agreed to call the Royal Yachting Society for advice. They told her that what we needed was a book called *The Ocean Passages of the World*. I said that I had that very book – but that it was in the office at home.

"Well why on earth didn't you take it with you?" she yelled down the line.

We had considered it, but it was a big, heavy book and we'd been desperately trying to cut down weight in the boat at the time. She sighed despairingly but promised to try to make sense of it.

A couple of hours later, having put our satellite position into the calculations suggested by the book, she called back.

"You're on a sort of curve," she said.

"Darling, I am in the middle of the Atlantic Ocean, what do you mean by a curve?" I asked, tired and frustrated by our situation.

"Right, I want you to imagine a young woman's body," came the reply. "Think of her hip bone as each side with the little tush in the middle as the bottom of the curve. That's where you are now – on that tush."

Fraser couldn't hear what Elaine was saying, but could see my eyes glazing over at the thought of a young woman's naked body after so many days at sea. Elaine researched wind patterns for us until it was clear that if we kept to a very tight course and didn't waver, we might just make it to Barbados at a pinch. Our slack decision-making at the critical moment had cost us many days of tough rowing, but now, thanks to Elaine, our hope was seemingly restored.

— • —

The incident was one in a growing litany of crazy decisions that we seemed to have made. We had decided, for example, to rely solely on dehydrated sachets of food throughout the voyage. These would save us valuable weight and it meant cooking would simply consist of using our solar-powered desalination filter to turn some seawater into drinking water, then boiling that in a kettle on a camping stove, before adding to the sachet and letting it stand for a few minutes.

Imagine our shock when we went to boil our first kettle of water, only to find that we had left it behind. After frantically rummaging around on the boat, we were fortunate enough to find another one, albeit a cheap mini-kettle from Woolworths, which was all that we had to boil our water in for the next nine and half weeks. How is it that you can sometimes think of everything except those that are crucial to survival?

We rowed in shifts of two hours on, two hours off through each 24-hour period to keep that boat moving towards Barbados. Ablutions were rare; toilet arrangements were basic. Everything had to be done in a constantly swaying, rolling environment, usually more wet than dry. The sea was wild, the tiny crawl-in cabin was cramped and the winds were often against us.

The nights were typically the worst. Many nights were starless, so Fraser and I had only the booming of surging waters and impenetrable darkness for company. We heard voices – or what we thought were voices – on the waves. If there was one thing that we needed, it was a sense of humour and, though it was often in abundance, there were also plenty of times when it was in short supply.

Deciding to take a swim on a calm day in the Atlantic, I looked back to take a picture of our boat and saw Fraser waving at me frantically. Shark, I thought. I swam back in panic, only to find it was a prank!

Six weeks in, I could tell that Fraser was starting to get in a bad way. He had gone very quiet and now completely lost his natural sense of fun. I started to get worried about him. I could see that at night he would sit staring, not rowing or rowing very little.

I didn't realise at the time that he had become quite frightened of the dark, and that he had started seeing images and hearing people calling out to him across the water, asking him to join them.

One night, he had even dreamed that Gollum from *The Lord of the Rings* was climbing into the boat with a large fish in his mouth. When I tried to talk to him about it, all he could tell me was that it was as if he constantly was looking down into a dark hole, which was drawing him in.

I called Elaine. She was, after all, a pharmacist and a counsellor – maybe she could help, even though we were thousands of miles away. She quickly directed me to the medical kit that she'd packed for us, with diazepam, giving me directions about the required dose.

The question was: would Fraser, the tough policeman who didn't believe in pills, take the medicine? I broached the subject while he was rowing, and telling him that I'd been tidying the medical box and found some happy pills – and that I was going to try them.

He hesitatingly agreed to it and we worked out a plan whereby, when it was time in the day to take them, we would dispense them to one another so that we didn't end up overdosing by accident. Whether it was the diazepam or the solace in imagining that *something* was on our side, Fraser pepped up – and I felt better for it myself.

In any race such as this, it is always going to come down to how well you can cope with the hardships and how quickly you can solve problems. Being able to make decisions under pressure turns out to be the fundamental difference between success and failure, or even life or death.

Our dilemma was handling the effects of being nearly constantly tired. Rowing consistently, and without respite, can make you feel as if your mind is grinding to a halt – and this compromises your ability to respond intelligently to the problems that you're facing. I was fortunate enough to be able to talk to Elaine on a fairly regular basis – typically, once every two days via our satellite phone – and she acted as a sort of sanity check for me, particularly in terms of some of the decisions that we were grappling with. Certainly, there were times when I spoke to her where I was so tired and confused that I would've struggled to spell my name correctly if she had asked.

In the lead-up to the race, I had been approached by Lew Hardy at Bangor University, asking whether Fraser and I would be interested in being lab rats for a study by his colleagues in the sports science department while on our transatlantic row. They were interested in seeing how we coped. Lew is an old friend so we agreed of course, and we even managed to persuade some of the other teams to participate, since it didn't involve much more than a series of interviews and questionnaires.

The feedback was telling. There was a general feeling among the rowers, during the early part of the race, that once you get to Cape Verde and go west, things would get much easier. Fraser and I had certainly had fantasies that from that point onwards, we would experience huge waves and wind driving us forward easily on target for Barbados.

But this was far from the truth. What's more, some rowers equally felt that, once you got close to Barbados, things would get easier. But they didn't: they just got harder. Reserves were running down and depression was setting in because, after so many days at sea, we were all more realistic about the *real* pain and *real* distance left to go.

Previous rowers had told us that very quickly, we would resort to rowing naked as all our clothes would end up drenched in either seawater or sweat, or both, and that we would be lucky if we didn't end up with a nasty, raw form of nappy rash.

Sure enough, this happened pretty quickly to us. The pain of sitting on a salt-encrusted rowing seat with a red, raw bum was horrendous. This was compounded by the intense pain in closing our fingers around the end of the oar as we took up our next rowing shift.

I had heard rowers talk about screaming for the first 30 seconds each time they started rowing, and now I understood why. After two hours of rowing, it would take a real effort to try and straighten out your fingers only to have to clench them around the oars again two hours later.

This continuous cycle is the nearest I can imagine to torture – and took all the resilience that I could muster to stick at it. One advantage of rowing with someone else in this respect is, of course, motivation – because if you are even 10 seconds late for taking over your shift, they'll let you know about it!

— • —

We had hoped to reach Barbados's northern coastline, but during the last week of our odyssey, we were concerned that we would continue being blown south and go past Barbados altogether. We were at our limits: our nerves frayed, stretched taut like a sail, our naked bodies – weathered by sun, wind and salt – exhausted; our hands fashioned into claws from the continuous clasping of the oars.

It was at its worst at night. Rogue waves would suddenly come from nowhere, pick up the end of an oar and flail it around, before breaching the side of the boat and battering into you.

Eventually, we found ourselves just a few miles offshore and heard what sounded like people's voices. We turned to see a brightly-coloured fishing boat nearby, its crew staring straight at us. I was so excited, not having seen another human being for the past nine weeks, that I stood up and shouted for them to come aboard for a cup of tea.

On hearing me hollering, Fraser awoke and crawled out of the cabin to join me. The guys on the boat just look puzzled, then amused and, turning away laughing, they quickly roared off. At that point, I looked down and suddenly realised that we had both been standing there stark naked. We must have looked like the victims of a shipwreck.

The crossing had turned out to be a bigger and more challenging undertaking than either of us had ever anticipated, but now, spurred on by the tantalising prospect that we might actually make it to the other side, that the dream could be realised, we held it together.

When we came into the harbour at Barbados, we had been rowing for 67 days and nights. At 58, I became the oldest Briton to have ever made the crossing and, together, Fraser and I entered something of a fringe pantheon of only 150 people on record who have been crazy enough to have rowed across an ocean. We were told after the event that our line of travel had been the straightest of any of the rowers – but it had to have been, I guess, because having got ourselves into dire straits south of Cape Verde, we knew that we couldn't let it slip an inch.

Land ho – arriving to Barbados after 67 days rowing across the Atlantic.

With Fraser in Barbados – still good friends after rowing for 3,000 miles.

— • —

At one point, I was being built up to be the oldest ocean rower ever at 58, but in the end a 60-year-old Russian called Pavel beat me to it. He had been rowing alone and had some amazing tales.

Pavel, like all of us, had planned to approach Barbados from the north then clip around into Port St Charles – the end of the race. The northern point of the island, however, is littered with rocks and for whatever reason, Pavel hadn't got the message from earlier rowers through the pass to keep well clear of them. He duly ended up with the bow of his rowing boat lodged on a protruding rock. He was too close to home to tolerate this.

In despair, he clambered down the side of his boat, put his back under the bow and, with all his strength, pushed upwards – the rough underside of the boat scraping his skin as the wet rock finally gave up its grip and the craft slipped back into the sea.

But having succeeded in dislodging it, he was now faced with another a problem: the boat was quickly drifting out to sea without him. He was forced to swim after it and, when he finally caught up with it, he faced the gruelling task of heaving himself up and over its steep side while constantly being buffeted by sea swell. It's a hard enough task when you have a partner to help you; a Herculean one when you're on your own. But Pavel did it and, having done so, quietly got on with rowing around the coast to the finish line at Port St Charles – becoming the oldest person ever to have rowed the Atlantic.

As we were celebrating in Barbados, I remember talking to Pavel and a young guy called Sam, who, at 23, had been the youngest person

So elated to have made it, I couldn't resist a victory dip.

to make the crossing. I asked Pavel if he thought he would have done anything like this when he was 23. In his broken English, he said no, he would never have had the courage at that age. I had turned to Sam and asked if he could imagine doing it again at Pavel's age.

"You must be joking," he'd said.

I guess that there is a time and a place in life for all of us. A time when, metaphorically, the stars align to clear us for take off on this or that adventure. Certainly, if someone had told me when I was 23 that I would be rowing the Atlantic just over a year before my 60th birthday, I would never have believed it possible.

SIXTEEN

Blistering Heat

Six marathons in seven days, across the Sahara desert. That was what I'd signed up for. The Marathon des Sables, I'd been told, was the "toughest footrace on earth": the event that defined the word ultramarathon. It can get as hot as 50 degrees Celsius out there, and don't even get me started on the sandstorms, a friend had said.

I'd also heard a lot about blisters. In fact, that was the one thing that everyone had agreed on: blisters – and how it was impossible not to get lots of them.

"Shit, this is going to be hard enough already at my age," I thought. "There must be a way to avoid getting blisters as well."

There is no doubt that as one gets older, the physical side of these events becomes much harder. Approaching the age of 60, I was already having to work harder and harder to keep fit. The mental side though, in a sense, was becoming more manageable, largely because I was prepared to have a more generous and less limiting definition of what success means. I was always going to be slower than many of the other runners, so I decided that my challenge was to be able to finish each day's miles and still feel like I could run the next day. Which brings me back to the blisters.

The Marathon des Sables or "marathon of sands" is a 156-mile footrace, set up in 1986 by Frenchman Patrick Bauer. Participants run a series of six marathons – though the longest stage could be up to 55 miles in a single day – through the Sahara while the sun beats down on them and the winds whip up the sands so that it gets *everywhere*.

The combination of unrelenting heat, sand grains that make it into your shoes and socks and the fact that each day you have to get up and run a marathon all over again, makes blisters almost inevitable. I was determined not to get any.

Through friends of friends, I tried to find everyone I could who had managed to complete the race without blisters. There weren't many, but there were a few – and I asked all of them to share with me exactly how they did it. I collated a list of about a half a dozen key things and decided that I would follow them religiously.

— • —

On the plane over to Morocco, a race organiser was briefing the British contingent. Among the list of instructions that he was working through, he made a throwaway remark about swimming.

"Look, when you get to the hotel today, make sure you really enjoy the pool, because when you get back from the race, you won't be able to use it."

Curious to know what it was that would put the pool out of action,

I went over to ask. "Blisters," he said. "It's because you'll have blisters and they don't want you to dirty the pool."

I asked him what would happen if I didn't have any and, without hesitation, he replied: "Oh you will. I can promise you, you will."

All right, well, imagine I don't have any blisters, I said to him, what will I need to do before I can get in the pool?

"You'll have to get a doctor's note confirming that it's safe for you to swim," he said.

I went back to my seat smiling. Before, I just didn't want to get any blisters, now I had a reason not to get any.

— • —

My primary goal was, of course, to get to the end of the race. To do this, I needed to make sure that I avoided being overtaken by one of the two camels that swept up the stragglers. If you saw a camel, you were advised to get a move on because, once it passed you, you were out of the race.

I was slightly concerned that the time-consuming routine I'd developed to protect my feet might end up costing me the race. Every couple of hours, I would stop, take off my two pairs of socks and swap them for fresh ones – hanging the sweaty pair off my rucksack to dry out as I ran. To be honest, the way that I had rigged up my footwear with gators made out of parachute silk and specialist shoes, it was hard to see how any sand was going to get near my feet, but, nevertheless, I stuck to the process.

By the end of day one, it was clear that it was paying off. As people completed each stage of the race they were led to the Médecins Sans Frontières tent. Here, French doctors and nurses would allegedly cut the loose skin from around their blisters and slap iodine all over them, at which point, you could usually hear the patient scream all the way from your own tent! Once patched up, the runners would be given a kind of shower cap to keep their feet clean, before they were then dropped off at their tents for the night.

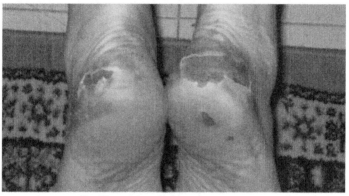

The blistered feet of a fellow competitor in the
notorious Marathon des Sables in 2005.

One of the guys who turned up at our tent was in a bad way. He was an ex-army officer from the Guards and he looked tough. Failure isn't really an option for the Guards, and you could tell that he still had that mentality. Having survived the merciless slapping on of iodine from the medics, he stumbled into our tent, which was essentially a black, sideless bivouac with a rug sheet on the ground. We got him some food and helped him into his sleeping bag.

At some point in the middle of the night, he must have needed a pee, because I remember waking in the shadows to see him crawling out of the tent on his hands and knees, unable to put any pressure on his feet.

At dawn the next morning, there was a frenzy of activity as local Bedouin tribesmen whisked away the black canvas of the tents that we were sheltered under, sending sand flying and waking everyone with a shock. This would happen every morning and, each time, all hell would break loose as people scrambled to repack their gear and get some food in before the race started.

I looked over to our friend from the Guards and thought surely he's never going to run today. He was sitting on the ground with a deeply pained expression as he unglued his weeping feet from the inside of his sleeping bag. But having successfully detached them, he slowly pulled on fresh socks and then his shoes. The whole process must have taken at least 20 minutes, all the while, I could see him grimacing as each sock went over his blisters. We helped him up with his kit and he hobbled over to the start line, one hand on my shoulder, the other clenched into a fist in pain.

It might seem counterintuitive to get everyone's heart rate up before running a marathon, but each morning the race organiser, which was usually Patrick Bauer himself, would whip everyone up into a frenzy with a stirring pep talk, music and singing. Of course, the more the event went on and the more exhausted we all became, the more the necessity of this rabble-rousing start became clear.

Eventually, we heard "Ready, steady, go!" and I watched as the Guard humbly set off into the distance with everyone else to run yet another marathon.

I stuck with him, day after day after day and, by the end of the race, the back of his foot was literally hanging off. But he never let it stop him.

— • —

In the end, I never did see a camel. In fact, much to my surprise, I completed the different phases of the race in respectable times, finishing about three-quarters through the pack. But the real reward for my efforts was still to come.

On the first morning back at the hotel, hundreds of runners descended on the swimming pool. None of them, of course, could use it, though – instead, everyone was forced to either hobble about or sit around on sun loungers, with their feet in bandages.

I gazed out at the empty pool with a smile on my face, a pass from the doctor burning a hole in the pocket of my swimming shorts. I dived in. It was the nicest length that I've ever swum.

SEVENTEEN
Pollarhuller: Not Me

The North Pole had never really interested me. I'd seen incredible-looking pictures of the Arctic of course, and I knew that for some people it could be an addictive place. There's even a Scandinavian word pollarhuller (literally someone with a hunger for the poles) to describe how once you've been to the Arctic, you will always want to go back.

I had felt that way about the desert. Ever since my first trip to Jordan in 2001 to do some rock climbing in Wadi Rum – the Valley of the Moon – I had been infatuated with the bare sandstone and granite cathedrals presiding over an otherwise empty landscape during the day and over starry skies full to bursting at night. Perhaps I would come to feel the same way about the Arctic if I went.

In 2008, I was doing some consultancy work and fell into conversation with a man named Phil Hayday-Brown, who happened to be involved in a business that took people to the North Pole. It was called Polar Challenge and, every year, the company organised a series of races out on the ice. I knew nothing about the Arctic at that point, other than that it was to be respected and that any expedition there could only be done with people who were far more skilled and experienced than me.

"What if I got a group of business people together and we came in to join one of your annual races?" I asked him.

I had some guys in mind and knew they would relish the opportunity to get trained up for something as daunting as this.

Phil was receptive, but cautious: we would need to talk logistics and risk. When you take senior business people who are highly depended on by their companies, there's the obvious insurance that you need to take out in case you get sued when someone catches frostbite or worse. We agreed that I'd find the people and come up with a price that was both financially viable for the candidates themselves and for me to take on the considerable risk of running the trip. I made the figures work and started assembling a team.

More by serendipity than design, I ended up with four guys in their late 40s – old enough to be experienced, but young enough to be fit and *get fitter* as we trained for the trip. Charles Hutton-Potts was a partner in a finance company, Jim Wilkinson was the chief finance officer at a gaming company, John Whalley ran a direct marketing company and Ed Bussey was a serial entrepreneur.

They all had young families or relationships that already suffered from time away from home, so my plan was for us to join a Polar Challenge race halfway through, giving us about 10 days to get to the North Pole and then get airlifted out. In the lead up, we would have just two weekend-long training blocks together; otherwise, everybody would have to be put their own training in and be honest with the rest of the group that they were pulling their weight, because once we were on the ice, there would be little margin for error.

— • —

The rain had started coming down around midday and hadn't stopped. Whole swathes of Cumbria had already been flooded. The team had already hauled a heavy boat up one mountain and down another; now it was dark and I was asking them to abseil down into an old flooded quarry and swim across it. Most of the four men had run marathons or played rugby at good levels; they were all keen skiers too, but this was a different type of a challenge for them.

Every time that they started looking relaxed, I cranked up the volume even more. The rain poured, the physical tasks got tougher and, all the while, they had to manage small intellectual tasks that demanded that they keep their focus in the bitter cold. But the harder it got, the better they were getting.

Eventually, having reached the other side of the quarry, they had to climb up and out through a tunnel, run along the road for a couple of miles and make camp for the night. All this had to be done against the clock, since in the Arctic, exhausted, with our body temperatures plummeting, we would need to get our tents up and the stove going in minutes.

This first training weekend in Lake District had given me confidence that all four of the guys were committed to the expedition and would pull together well once we were out there. Before we had left the Lakes, we had done an intense feedback session, where each of them were asked to give their views on each other. I had been impressed by how open they were compared to some other senior business people that I'd coached. We worked through some psychometric profiling to help them understand how they might each behave when under the arduous conditions of the Arctic, and again I was impressed. The next step was to get them on some snow.

— • —

Some months before we were due to fly into the race, we headed to Norway to find what it was going to be like to ski while dragging a sledge – or *pulk*, as they're called. It was at this stage that I began to realise how tough this was going to be. When you were going uphill, the pulks would drag back behind you, toppling you off balance; only to then chase you down the other side, biting at your ankles.

They proved to be incredibly difficult to get under control. I remember being quite exhausted during the training, wondering whether it was simply because I wasn't a prolific skier, but even those who were admitted to finding it tough. The result was to make everyone nervous that they might somehow let the team down when the time came. The only way to overcome this fear was by training at home, so that's what we did.

When we arrived back in England, I told everyone to get hold of some heavy tyres. Stringing two or three together on a length of rope, which you then attached to a harness, was the best way to simulate the exertion of dragging a sledge. And they really did slow you down.

I was dragging these tyres through Epping Forest for about six months for about two hours at a time – sometimes in snow, but mostly on wet, boggy forest floor, or dry trail if I was lucky. Horses would rear up, dogs would try to attack them, but eventually people got used to seeing me with my harness on and my strange cargo.

The other guys got stuck in and found that they loved the training – it gave them something unusual to talk about in the pub.

"He's running with tyres at the weekend!"

"He's going to the North Pole!"

While, inevitably, the time taken up with training could be hard for partners and families, to not put the hours in could jeopardise our chances once on the ice. Something that would quickly become clear.

— • —

Resolute Bay in Ottawa, Canada, is a well-known staging post for North Pole races. We arrived one evening in April and the next morning were out on the ice for the first of two days of training with Polar Challenge before we would be dropped into the race.

In those two days, they drilled into us all the essential skills that we needed to know. Nothing was left to chance. They ran it like a military operation: there was only one way to do things and that was the right way. If you didn't, you were likely a dead man, or worse, if a polar bear had anything to do with it. There were always aspects of any adventure that I had been on that needed to be taken deadly seriously, but there was something about the Arctic, something about the cold, unforgiving and isolated landscape that we were going out into that made this different.

Chatting to the race organiser, he'd told me that he'd seen seasoned mountaineers and endurance athletes, who trained for the North Pole, get off the plane at Resolute Bay only to be so shocked by the blast of ice cold air that they had withdrawn from the challenge within hours. Usually my excitement balances out or, typically, overrides any apprehension that I have before an expedition, but this time was different: I was worried that I might let the team down somehow.

My fears were compounded when, at the last minute, the Twin Otter plane that was due to take us into our starting point couldn't take off. We were held at base camp for about a day and a half while the weather cleared, which had serious implications for our time on the ice. By day 10 we needed to be at the Pole with all the other teams in order to catch our plane home, and if we weren't we could expect a penalty fee of some £30,000 for a second flight to come out for just one team. We were going to be under pressure to move quickly from the outset.

I would be sharing a tent with Ed and Phil, who'd been the catalyst for the adventure in the first place; with Charles, John and Jim in the other tent. We'd move as two separate groups, linking up via the radio and camping within a reasonable distance of each other each night. At the last moment, Phil was pulled into a logistical emergency that would mean he had to stay at base camp. All of sudden, the team that we had become accustomed to was dismantled and we would have a last-minute replacement.

Gary was an ex-Marine and apparently an expert in Arctic warfare. He was young, fit and ruthlessly efficient. There was nothing he didn't know about this environment, which was reassuring, but it made it no less intimidating to be sharing a tent with him.

— • —

We set off. Every day for 12 hours, we would drag the pulks over the sea ice, through fields of ice boulders that the pulks would get caught on, causing you to fall over. It was infuriating. At times, we would have to climb up and over small islands, perhaps some 300-foot high; in boots, they would have been no trouble at all, but in skis they were a nightmare. And it didn't get any better going down the steep, undulating sides as you tried to avoid getting knocked over by your own sledge.

In fact, if there's one thing I remember of those first few days, it's falling over. Again and again and again. It was incredibly wearing on the body – and the patience. It just seemed impossible to find a rhythm!

Every hour, Gary would call us to a halt and say, "Right, we're going to stop here for eight minutes – so you've got eight minutes to do whatever it is you need to do".

We'd rack our three pulks up next to each other, drop our skis back so that we could sit on a pulk and then Gary would pull a cover around us to form a temporary storm shelter.

We performed this routine meticulously, on the hour, every hour we were walking. As soon as time was up, Gary would whip the cover away and we were on the march again. I had never experienced such a tightly-run ship on any expedition that I'd been on – there was no time to stop and take photos. You were constantly on the move.

This was partly my doing. Yes, we were up against the clock to get to the Pole before our plane left, but I had also told the organisers that I wanted them to push us, since my guys had specifically asked me to put create a tough adventure for them. For safety's sake, you couldn't really afford to hang around anyway. The teams in front of us had faced horrendous weather – this was the reason that we were kept at base camp for that extra day and a half – and this had mostly cleared by the time we were on our way. But what we gained in clear skies, we paid for in fiercely cold temperatures.

If you stopped and stood still, you instantly got cold, so you had to get under cover as soon as possible in order to retain body heat. The simplest tasks were complex rituals: if you took your glove off, tucked it under your arm and let it somehow to drop to the floor, it would blow away and you'd never see it again. You had to keep your kit as light as possible, so you only had a limited number of spares – do it again and you could be in serious trouble. And if your fingers were exposed for more than a couple of minutes, you'd get frostbite and your race could be over. We had already heard that the organisers had pulled some teams out because they wouldn't let them continue with frostbitten fingers or toes.

Clearly, this was not a place to experiment. Before we'd left, we'd even been drilled on what to do in the event of encountering a polar bear at close quarters. This was treated very seriously. One man per team was in charge of a gun – a Remington pump action shotgun – and, at all times, he had to keep the sheath open and the safety off.

All the teams in the race would be trekking along a passage dubbed Polar Bear Alley, where 80 per cent of the planet's polar bears reside – and they would smell us long before we could see them.

For one of the race leaders, this drill would later prove to be invaluable. Having stopped to check his glove on his right hand, he suddenly caught a glimpse of something in the corner of his eye. He turned to look and there, a hundred metres away but closing fast, was a 13-foot polar bear.

Fortunately, he was the shotgun carrier and having whipped the gun out, he now swung it at the bear. The problem was that – as we'd all been taught – it's a criminal offence to actually shoot to kill these animals. You can be taken to court and heavily fined. So he followed the exact procedure: he fired over its head, then to the left of it, then to the right.

It was still coming, and he had only one more shot left. He fired at the bear's feet. The bullet hit the ice and sent a spray of ice up into the bear's face, causing it rear up on its hind legs in shock. Miraculously, it was enough – the bear stopped its advance and sloped off.

When, much later, I had a chance to chat to the guy, he said that he had measured the distance between where he had been standing and where the bear's claw marks had finished. It was a matter of metres. The bear had approached him silently, he said, and he had been "really lucky" that he'd checked his glove when he did.

I remember laughing when he said he'd been lucky because that, for me, epitomises a survivor. Most people would say, "How unlucky that guy was! He was nearly eaten by a polar bear!"

— • —

The constant pressure of minute-by-minute routines was starting to get to me. I had come across plenty of people in the past – disciplined, well-organised, focused people – who would have excelled in these conditions, but I was beginning to doubt whether I had what it took. Perhaps for the people who had been in the race from the start, who were now approaching four or five weeks on the ice, it had become second-nature to them, but for us it felt like the learning curve was steep. Too steep?

We couldn't afford to lose concentration – constantly having to watch where you were going, making sure that you were keeping up with the team, thinking ahead. Every now and then you'd take over the lead, which meant getting an accurate reading from the GPS while trying not to fall over. It was coming up to my turn again as we were ascending what felt like a mountain beneath the ice, when I hit the wall.

"John, you can lead from here," Gary yelled through the wind, handing me the GPS. I took it from him and fumbled trying to get a bearing. As I was about to set off in the direction that I thought we should be going in, I noticed Gary and Ed were taking a different route. Oh Christ, I'm going the wrong way, I thought. I caught up to them, exhausted:

"Gary, do me a favour, will you? Take the lead. I'm doing as much as I can to keep up with everyone right now and if I lead, we're just going to waste time."

He hesitated and gave me a funny look, but eventually said, "All right, OK then".

But as he turned away, I heard him mutter to Ed, "I thought we were going to get a 'refusing to soldier' then!"

If you've been in the military, you'll know that that's a very serious phrase to use. "Refusing to soldier" is the most debasing thing that you can ever have levelled against you and, when I heard it, it struck me like a punch to the gut. I reeled, and thought, "You bastard. I'm trying my damned hardest here. Just give me a hand."

But I don't think sympathy counted for much in Gary's book, so I just fell in behind him and kept moving.

Eventually, we made it down the other side of the hill onto easier ground and racked up the pulks. I asked if they could wait a minute while I recorded a short video diary.

Trying to keep it together during a trek to the North Pole in 2010.

I stepped out of earshot and started talking into the camera about how I was feeling. For the past few hours, I had been dwelling on what it meant for a leader to have stepped away from their leadership role. Clearly, Gary thought my decision had been unacceptable, whereas I felt that, if you're leading and you're feeling rough, it's not a clever thing to carry on leading. Or was I just post-rationalising the situation I now found myself in?

I remember talking this through on my little diary and thinking, "Sod it, you're going to get back out there and lead".

I finished up the recording, got up and told Gary that I wanted to take my turn.

I struck off at a really fast pace – so much so that he eventually had to say: "Slow down man!" But I couldn't; I felt fired up and angry, and it was spurring me on.

"How dare you," I kept saying in my mind, "you're 30 years younger than me – be a bit more sympathetic."

We forged on, eventually catching up to the other team, who were just starting to strike camp.

— • —

Putting a tent up in the Arctic is never easy. We had a routine and Gary would kick your arse if you were slow: he and Ed would get the frame and outer tent up, then, the moment it was up, I'd dive in and set out all the inside before starting to get our food ready. By this time, the two of them would be back with big bags of snow for me to melt on the stove. The whole process would take no longer than 10 minutes.

Once we were inside, it was imperative to keep your kit well organised; in such a confined space, anyone making a mess would disrupt everyone else. We would cook on MSR camp stoves, which are highly effective at boiling water in the cold but, because they're petrol-fuelled, can be extremely dangerous. So we were always on tenterhooks around these stoves, and for good reason – if they flare up, they tend to take the tent and everything else with them.

On the third day, Ed was boiling some water when he turned his back on the stove to take a call on the satellite phone. Instantly, it flared up. Gary grabbed the nearest thing to hand, which happened to be my jacket, smothered the flames and had the stove out of the tent in what could only have been seconds. If he hadn't, the whole tent would have gone up and we would have been left with nothing.

I was hugely impressed with how Gary leapt forward and saved the day, but by now the atmosphere had soured for me. I felt as if I had been slowing the team down and his hard-hearted attitude only served to compound my anxiety. And it wasn't even that we had been going *that* slowly, we just had to catch this damn plane. In fairness to the rest of the team, no one ever chided me for my speed, but I seemed to be trapped in a negative feeling that was made worse by how exhausted I was. I wished I was 20 years younger.

Gradually, the days blurred into one. The sun never rose or set – we were treated to a state of permanent daylight. And as glorious and ethereal as that sometimes was, it plays havoc with your body clock. Instead of sleeping for a block of eight hours, we slept for a few hours here and there before we got moving again.

On our eighth day on the ice, we got a call from the organisers.

"Whatever happens guys, you've got to get to the North Pole and the finish line tomorrow – the plane is now waiting for you."

This was incredibly serious: we knew that this was nearly impossible for us to do with the distance we still had left to cover. But we had to get there; we knew the financial penalties and it would've been wrong to say, "Sod it, send another plane!"

We got both teams together; and after a short, fitful sleep, we got up and resolved to make a bid for the finish line and the plane home in a single, final push.

— • —

The North Pole, it turns out, is very disappointing. There's nothing there – just a bit of flat ice and the blip blip of a GPS reading telling you that you're there. And that's the Magnetic North Pole. The solo adventurers that you hear about tend to go the Geographic North Pole, which sits in the middle of the Arctic Ocean. It's a longer, more perilous journey over unstable sea ice that can, and frequently does, open up to create canals of water in front of you.

In hindsight, I'm not sure what I had expected to find there, but it's overwhelming nothingness seemed to reinforce the sense of isolation that the Arctic imbues – or perhaps simply had imbued in me on this trip, this time, at this stage of my life. It would be wrong to say that I took nothing from that moment, of course, but time was still against us, so after stopping briefly to savour the triumph of having reached one of the most sought-after and dreamt-about spots on the planet, we ploughed on.

A few miles from the North Pole, there is a military base with outhouses and a runway, and that was to be our finish line. Those final hours were relentless. I had taken the lead and was pushing hard, but as we neared our target, I was struggling to stay at the front.

John later told me that I was veering about all over the place as if drunk, my eyes glazed over, gone, like a robot simply putting one foot in front of the other. I can barely remember – but as we settled into our seats in the plane, a sense of relief washed over me: I hadn't seriously held the team up, we had made the plane and, thankfully, it was all over.

— • —

When I look back on the experience, I know that all the guys who came away on the expedition had a great time. And that's wonderful, because, ultimately, that is my job. We still talk about it now when we meet up. I have a video of John showing us his foot at the end of the trip where a huge blister (which he'd had from day one) had ground away down to the bone. But he'd just kept pushing on, pushing through the pain, day after day. I've got huge respect for how all of them handled themselves.

A lot of the credit for making it a success goes to Gary, too. He had to be hard on us, had to push us to reach that plane on time. Yet I could never shake the feeling that he looked down on me.

When we had got back, I had sent him a few emails – some photos, a note of thanks – but he never replied. I think he knew I'd been an army officer and, in his mind, I was a "Rupert": a name that soldiers sometimes give to officers who they think are out of touch, from a different world to themselves.

It had been the first time for a long time that I had been involved in an expedition that I wasn't leading and, on reflection, I found that difficult to cope with. If that sounds like a hunger for power, it's not – it's that when you're leading you have a sense of purpose: you have to keep everything together, make sure your teammates are happy and inspire in them the same sense of purpose. That in itself is very rewarding.

To be plodding endlessly to points on a map I found a bit soul-destroying. And unlike other expeditions that I'd been on – particularly climbing expeditions – where there were always times when you were waiting, and could look at the view, watch the other guy and wait your turn, or just spend some time nurturing that sense of purpose, there was never a time in the Arctic where you could relax and feel off-duty. That's how cruel that environment is. At least, I know now what I had perhaps always known – that it wasn't for me.

EIGHTEEN

Know Your Limits

I felt about a hundred years old. There, in the first light of dawn, some miles inland from the Skeleton Coast, I shuffled uncomfortably, adjusting the shoulder straps of my pack – I'm carrying far too much weight for a serious race like this, I thought. The starting pistol fired and all around me runners launched themselves forward. This feels *fast*, I thought.

After less than a mile, it dawned on me that I had made the wrong decision to enter this event. I couldn't have caught these runners up even if I was running flat out and I was looking down the barrel of another 24 hours of this.

The Namibia 24-hour Ultramarathon was the first time that I knew for sure that I was getting older. It seemed like only a few years before that I had successfully – and enjoyably – completed the 156-mile Marathon des Sables. This was a race of half that distance, albeit still the length of three marathons in one day. I had loved the gathering of runners at the campsite the previous day and the organisation that was running the event – Across the Divide – had given a stirring briefing. But this morning, the morning where it really counted, my enthusiasm had started to melt away, leaving only nerves.

I had done a fair amount of training in the UK, but it was clear to me now that the other racers were on another level. They look young, fit and were wearing all the latest ultramarathon gear. 'The latest gear' is not something that typically makes me anxious, but here it was patently a symbol of investment not just of money but of time, experience and hard work in preparing to come here, to a desert on the edge of the world and do something special.

— • —

The distance between me and the last runner in front of me was growing wider and wider and, in the brightness of the early morning sun, I was struggling to see the marker signs for the route. Like the other competitors, I had inputted the way markers into my GPS, but now I could not seem to make sense of it – the route was a curve, but I seemed to heading straight out. My rucksack, which I had used to great effect during the Marathon des Sables, now felt awkward and cut into my shoulders. I felt weak, my resolve was ebbing away and I'd barely even started.

A couple of hours into the race, I came into the first checkpoint a full 10 minutes after the last runners. The organisers looked at me – or at least I felt like they were – as if to say, "What are you doing in an event like this?"

They warned me that I was getting seriously close to being timed out and that this was only the first of many checkpoints. I mumbled something about having got lost, said I would be better once I got going, but knew I had nothing in the tank.

I set off down the long, hot, boring road in the sand. I got out of sight of the checkpoint and started to walk. This is ridiculous I said to myself, you've got to get out of this nightmare. It struck me that I would be far happier helping the people who were running the event than I would be running in it.

Could I pull out of the race and reframe things somehow? As I walked that road, kicking dust and berating myself for entering the event so unprepared, I worked out that the happiest thing for me that day would be to offer myself up to the organisers to help support other runners at the various checkpoints along the route.

A huge, five-tonne truck came up behind me. Desert races always have a "sweeper", a guy whose job it was to pick up any casualties or runners who'd timed out, and in this case it was Faarn – a tough, old Namibian about my age. I flagged him down and he climbed out of the cabin and came over to me.

"The race is over for me this year," I said.

It was a relief to hear myself say it out loud, though he looked shocked that anyone would pull out so early on. I explained I was sure about my decision and gave him my proposal. After a couple more minutes in which Faarn satisfied himself that I really was serious, he happily agreed. I jumped into the cab and we trundled off through the sand.

— • —

It wasn't long before we were passing streams of runners. Twenty minutes from where Faarn had picked me up, we passed two young runners being treated for sunstroke by a medical team. They had gone off too fast.

By the time we got to the halfway mark, runners were dropping like flies. Some of them were lying about like corpses on drips, while some, dehydrated and fatigued, were looking worried as they told the medics that their pee was turning dark brown with blood.

We drove on, each new checkpoint resembling more a military casualty operation than a race. I did what I could to keep up the morale of flagging runners – convincing some of them that this wasn't, in fact, the end of their race but the start of it, that as the dusk drew in and the temperature dropped, they could make good time while it was cooler. Their problem now, of course, would be keeping warm as the cold sea mist from the Skeleton Coast swept in, pushing the temperature down further.

I stood at the finish the next morning; watching as they staggered over the line within the 24-hour cut-off was emotional. Following them through the night, I had become very fond of them – not just the individuals I spoke to, but collectively – as inspiring men and women testing their limits, fighting on.

With the final runners in, we were all picked up and taken back to Windhoek – where we repaired to a glorious beach bar on the edge of the Atlantic coast. I made my way across the bar to congratulate the winner of the race: an Irishman with a drip attached to one arm and a pint of lager in the other.

Everyone was grinning from ear to ear, embracing, laughing. They had been through something together and that shared experience had bonded them tighter than glue. I could see the attraction and felt lucky to be in their company; because I had helped them when they needed it most, they had forgiven me for dropping out of the race and welcomed me into the fold.

— • —

I resolved that I would come back to Namibia again the following year. Not to attempt the ultramarathon – I had realised, perhaps with some relief, that this was by now way out of my league – but the single desert marathon race. This started at the same point as all the other runners but finished at the "one marathon" distance checkpoint.

That winter I trained hard – I ran longer, hillier distances in the forest, worked harder in the gym, and I found someone who could teach me the skills of speed walking. What I needed, I had realised, wasn't more speed but a steady pace that I could maintain over the distance.

Speed walking is an event in itself, but I just wanted to know enough so that I could move at almost the same speed as a slow runner, but with a lot less effort and fewer injuries. My final trick was to get hold of some extremely lightweight walking poles that could also be tucked into my rucksack when I wasn't using them.

— • —

On a cool May morning in 2010, we gathered for the start of the race, as we had done a year before. I was ruthlessly well-organised this year: I was carrying only the essentials and knew exactly how many calories and how much water would sustain me. I felt leaner and fitter and, most importantly, calmer, than last year. I knew that I would make it this time – even if I crawled in.

The gun sounded and the runners around me again took off at mind-boggling pace. I would be lying if I said I wasn't tempted to try and chase after the pack, but I resisted, and started to speed walk.

Around the 10-mile point, I started to see some runners who had dropped off the pace and were slowing almost to a walk. It felt good to be closing the gap. Periodically, they would turn around and, seeing me advancing on them, would break into a run again – for a while, at least.

Respecting my limits and succeeding on my
second ultramarathon in Namibia in 2009.

As the finish got ever closer, I pulled out my secret weapon – the walking poles – and started to propel myself on, picking up the pace. Some of the runners later told me that it felt like they were being chased by Robocop as they heard my sticks click-clacking behind them.

I held my arms aloft as I crossed the line, exultant, letting the self-discipline of the past hours and the previous 12 months drop away. The marathon had been a dream: I had finished in a good time and, more importantly, loved every minute of it. I had designed what success was going to mean for *me* and put myself in the best possible position to make it happen. I was just thrilled it had come off.

NINETEEN
The Guide

After more than a 30-year hiatus, I decided that it was time to revisit the Alps. I called an old friend of mine and mountain guide called Harold Edwards and asked if he'd like to accompany me. I wanted to climb the Matterhorn again, I said.

I had spent much of the late 1990s and early 2000s working with Harold up in the Lake District, where I continued to use Derwent Folds as a base for much of the leadership development work that I'd be doing since leaving the police. More often than not, he would be the first person that clients would meet: they'd spill out of the minibus, after what was often a seven-hour drive up from London, and we'd send them straight out on the crags with Harold.

He is a modest, principled man, with two main loves in his life: climbing and his wife. He accepted my offer of a trip to the Matterhorn, but said that work commitments would mean that we'd miss the ideal summer shot at an ascent. In the end, we didn't find ourselves on the road until September.

— • —

After about 12 hours in the car, we arrived in Chamonix to be greeted, this time, by a fine sunny day, with the deep blue skies that are only possible at higher altitudes. Having dumped our stuff at the chalet, we set off into the foothills outside the town to get a taste of what awaited us.

Immediately, I had to fight hard to keep up with Harold's pace. At 66, neither of us were spring chickens, but he is a whippet of a man, without an inch of fat on his lean frame. While he danced his way up to the start of the first long climbs like a mountain goat, I stumbled behind.

We roped up and continued to move easy for the next few hours. My rope work was rusty and it was becoming increasingly obvious that my agility had dropped off considerably in the intervening years. One of the problems with getting older is that it happens gradually; like the shortening days as the winter creeps in, you know it's there, but you tend not to see it coming!

These days much of my training consists not of scaling tough routes, but running or speed walking through the forest where I live. I have been covering the same route for the past 30 years or so. Some days it takes longer than others. Depending on what I am training for at the time, I might drag a tyre behind me in a harness or carry a 40-pound rucksack, but, in essence, it is an hour and half's-worth of hardy hills and muddy bogs that has always served me well.

Very often, I can run for a whole session without seeing a soul. I rarely take a watch and have never worked out how fast I run; rather, I slip into a kind of trance in which I am absorbed by the forest itself.

Over the years, I have come to see this retracing of the same loop as invaluable, as it is probably the only time that I really relax. Often, it is here, in my own little bit of wild country, that I dream up new ideas and adventures, and find that my mind is able to solve previously intractable problems.

It is only when I get together with good mountain guides like Harold that I realise how much faster and agile they are than me. This becomes particularly apparent when it comes to travelling downhill at speed, which was once my forte.

I used to be fearless, trusting the strength of my legs implicitly to keep me safe and alive. I don't have that confidence any more. Rather, I feel myself drifting imperceptibly towards a state where what I consider to be dashing would to anyone else be considered hobbling. I would have to be especially carefully on the way down this time round, I thought.

One of the lessons that climbing teaches you the hard way is that almost all accidents tend to take place after reaching the summit.

As a young man of 25, I'd been made keenly aware of this on a trip with Elaine up Striding Edge on Helvellyn. She had hated every minute of it and, as she sat on the path crying, terrified of descending further, I remember thinking that I must never put her, or anyone else, in this position again. But we still had to get down.

As I passed along a narrow ledge with a wall of rock to my right, I turned to my left to see how she was getting on and my rucksack struck the wall, throwing me off balance. I teetered on my toes for what seem like eternity, my insides drawn tightly against my spine, desperate to resist the inertia that wanted to topple me, until I was finally able to glue myself back to the wall. I was extremely grateful that in all the hazardous expeditions that I've been on in my life since then, that was still the closest I had come to falling 1,000 feet to my death.

— • —

These thoughts played on my mind the next morning, as Harold and I started into the mountains proper for a warm-up climb. Harold had chosen a route that would involve a complete traverse of a peak called Aiguille de la Perseverance and one called Aiguille des Chamois Integrale. It had been a while since Harold had climbed it, so we spent the first hour stumbling two steps forward, one step back on a shale slope of loose scree and boulders. As we finally arrived at the bottom of the route and looked up at the sheer face above us in the baking heat of the morning sun, I felt weak, pathetic and nervous. This was the opposite of being "in flow" like I had felt some 30 years earlier, but I didn't have too much time to dwell on it. Harold was soon off and I was paying out the rope below.

I had learned that when he stopped or slowed down on a climb, things are either getting difficult or about to get difficult, and that hand or footholds would be sparse. I watched his every move, trying to remember the pattern that he made on the rock so that I could replicate his ascent.

When it was my turn to try, I took a moment to remind myself to put my trust in the rope, that speed and focus were paramount, since hanging around was not an option on a long climb in September with the nights drawing in. Bit by bit, I zoned out, letting my body feel the way. The old days were back: I was "in flow".

By the time that we reached the summit, I was feeling quite emotional. The route was graded *Assez Difficile*, which was right at the top of the range of climbs that I had done in the past. Harold was pleased with my progress and that seemed to bode well for our attempt at the Matterhorn in a couple of days.

We made our way back to the refuge hut where we'd left the rest of our gear the night before to find that last cable car would be leaving in less than an hour and that we would be unlikely to make it. I remembered a similar set of circumstances 30 years ago. "Come on Harold, let's chance it," I said, knowing full well that it would mean running all the way down to the station.

Returning to climb the Matterhorn again after a 30-year hiatus.

Breathless, we made it with two minutes to spare. I slumped doggedly into the cable car, tired but elated that all those hours spent training in the forest were still doing the trick.

— • —

Before we had left England, Harold had warned me that a successful ascent of the Matterhorn was totally dependent on three things: the weather, our fitness and our technical competence. And now, it was the weather that was troubling him.

I suggested that we made our way across from Chamonix to Zermatt and then worked our way up to the refuge at the base of the Hornli Ridge at 10,700 feet to wait out the worst of it – just as I had done 30 years before. Harold agreed, but was reluctant to spend too much time up there – for one, it was bloody expensive on the Swiss side and two, in bad weather, it was a pretty dismal place to while away the time.

We arrived at the hut around midday and, after dropping off some of our kit, decided to do a reconnaissance of the first part of the climb. Anyone who has attempted the Matterhorn will tell you that most people fail to achieve their goal because they spend too much time trying to find the route on the lower section. There used to be a rumour that Swiss guides would even deliberately create false trails to send novice climbers off track.

As we pushed on up into the mist that shrouded the mountain that day, using the fixed ropes to steady ourselves over boulders and loose rock, we searched out the route, trying to mark it as best we could with small piles of stones.

The higher we got, the more soft uncompacted snow we encountered. This would make things even more unpredictable, so we decided to back off and return the following morning.

As we were retracing our steps to base camp, we bumped into a group of Eastern European climbers who had lost their way. We offered to lead them down to the hut, where they explained that they were returning from an unsuccessful bid for the top. One of them, who had already climbed Mont Blanc in the days before, looked shaken up.

"It's really quite bad up there," he said.

— • —

Despite the warning, we resolved to attack the Matterhorn again the following morning. About three quarters of the way up, we reached Solvay – a precarious mountain hut with no more than a metre-wide rock edge around the two sides from which you approach it. Normally, the views from here would be quite spectacular, but today the weather was pressing in.

As we arrived, a mountain rescue helicopter landed, allowing couple of guys to pick up some kit from the shed.

"Where are you going from here?" one of them asked.

"I thought we'd get a lift in your helicopter!" I said.

Judging by the disparaging looks he gave me, this was no time for joke.

"We're heading back down," Harold chimed in. "The conditions are too bad".

This was clearly the right answer.

"Good move. Snow melt is already making it tough going, but when it freezes to ice, it'll be even worse. Besides that, you could run short of daylight and have to descend in the dark."

As far as we had come and as badly as I wanted to summit the Matterhorn again after all these years, I was secretly delighted that the decision had been made for us. Now, all we had to do was get down.

A couple of Americans who had been right behind us on the ascent, now joined the conversation. We chatted with one of them who was also a mountain guide and had climbed the Matterhorn several times.

He reassured us that down was the direction we needed to be going – these were the worst conditions he had ever experienced up here. To speed up the descent, he suggested that we team up and use both our ropes so that we could abseil in 100-metre sections.

I led the abseils all the way down. At times, it was a serious challenge to find a good place for the next peg at the bottom of the rope, so it was a relief when we all arrived back in Hornli, safe and sound.

— • —

That evening in the hut, I was struck by the fact that there were a thousand times on that mountain where you could have slipped and fallen, and how totally dependent on your guide you were for stopping your fall. Until that moment, I don't think I had realised what serious risks mountain guides take every day in order to make it possible for people like myself to have such fulfilling experiences. They are an honourable and courageous bunch of people, and very much the unsung heroes of a sport that is not short of peak baggers and false prophets.

I hoped that something akin to a guide was the role that my team and I fulfilled in some of the work that we had started doing with inner-city youth workers, who we took away on wilderness survival programmes.

For many of them, the remote outdoors is an entirely new experience and it is an honour to witness the first time they conquer something new. When those guys go home, they take that with them and go on to do phenomenal things in their own lives.

For me, that's 10 times more rewarding that anything you can do on your own.

TWENTY

Sisyphus And The Beating Sun

The cabin lights dimmed and the engine droned on, as the South African airbus flew on through the night to its destination. I had tried to drift off but it was hopeless. We would be landing at Johannesburg Airport in a matter of hours and my mind was tormented by an awesome feeling of responsibility for what lay ahead.

From Jo'burg, we would connect with another flight on to Windhoek in Namibia and, from there, make our way on local buses into Damaraland in the north-western Namib Desert and the Brandberg Mountains.

I looked around at the rest of my group who were fast asleep and wondered if they too were worried; one or two knew the nature of the terrain that we were heading into, others were likely basking in the innocence of having never seen it first hand.

I'd led a similar expedition to the Brandberg Mountains the year before, and it had concluded with a long and nightmarish climb out of the Tisab Gorge. We had expected the climb to take three or four days, but it had taken six and we had nearly died of thirst in the 40-degree sun, having run our water supplies dry.

It had only been the enormous personal resilience of our local Namibian guide, Kobus, that had saved us. On the sixth night, he had set out down the mountain alone in search of water, returning at dawn with three gallons that he had managed to carry back up with him from a watering hole. With a group of 10 people, this year it would not be so easy to replenish supplies if ours ran out again.

At 8,550 feet at its tallest point, the Brandberg range is not particularly high, but the journey is arduous. The name is Afrikaans for "Fire Mountain", for the way that it glows in the setting sun, but might just as easily describe the sensation of burning under its gaze as you ascend its dry, rocky slopes.

Since that last visit in October 2011, a year had passed and no rain had fallen on the mountains to restock the meagre supplies in the various pools or "fountains", as the locals call them, which are scattered around on the mountain. We had also chosen to attack the mountain via a new route, the Numas Gorge.

The gorge was longer than our approach the previous year and, although it was meant to lead to a plateau on top from which we could then descend the other side, nobody that we spoke to seemed to know what the territory was like up there.

To hedge our bets, we anticipated that we would find no water on the route until we were halfway down the descent on day four, so we planned to carry 20 litres of water each on our backs, as well as provisions for up to five days' survival. I had told the team that they needed to think of the challenge as a plane crash situation: we'd crashed on one side of the mountain, but safety was on the other side and, since we had no idea what to expect in the middle, we'd need to carry everything that we could to be self-sufficient.

My mind continued to whir. What if one of the team members was to fall ill or get seriously injured on the mountain? How would we get them out alive? How would the rest of the team survive with the meagre water supplies while we were waiting for a rescue team to come in?

In the past, I'd carried injured climbers out of the mountains in North Wales and knew only too well the enormous effort that it took to move a stretcher over rough ground. This was the desert.

— • —

The transit at Jo'burg passed without incident, but on arrival at Windhoek, we were greeted with the news that a man had died on the Brandberg the previous day from dehydration and exhaustion. The rescue party had been unable to reach him and took a long time to get his body back off the mountain.

We were given the news by the local immigration officials as they stamped our passports, shaking their heads solemnly as they read our visas marked for the same place.

At Windhoek, we were united with the rest of the team, some of whom had flown in from other parts of the world the day before. As ever, it was a joy to receive a giant bear hug from Kobus. Kobus is a white Afrikaner in his mid-40s who looks like a cross between Crocodile Dundee and Indiana Jones. He has a mischievous sense of humour and is one of the warmest and most enthusiastic characters I've ever met.

We'd first encountered each other during the Namibian ultramarathon several years ago and, ever since, I'd been determined to find a way to work with him. He had spent his life in the bush, as a hunter and, later, game park warden running safaris.

At the ultramarathon, he had turned up in a worn-out T-shirt, a tired old pair of shorts, brown suede boots and a small satchel with just enough room for his pipe and tobacco. He'd barely seemed to drink any water throughout the 20 or so hours of the event, despite the baking desert sun, and having strolled over the finish line, lit his pipe to celebrate. After our expedition the previous year, I knew Kobus was the man who I wanted beside me as our guide.

I'd also teamed up with a young Swede called Joakim. We had planned the previous year's attempt together and, like me, he too had fallen in love with the Namibian wilderness and been determined to return.

Always the life and soul of the party, Joakim also has a tenderness that reveals itself as a profound interest in caring for other people. He is a pleasure to be around, and is an intensely fit man. Just three weeks before coming to Namibia, he had completed one of his 100-odd mile races through the Malaysian jungle and had arrived at the finish unscathed, in less than 24 hours.

A few months before departure, Joakim had approached me about whether his father, Borje, might be able to join the expedition. I'd been chatting to him about a new venture that I wanted to get under way called Father & Sons Adventures and it had piqued his interest. Though he himself already had a close relationship with his father, he was fascinated by the possibility that they could do an extreme adventure together.

I'd spoken briefly to Borje over Skype, but the language barrier had made it hard to get to know him well. The moment that I met him at the airport, though, I knew that he was going to be a good team player and his innate sense of humility made everyone instantly warm to him. Borje was 68 years old – one year older than me at the time, but had trained hard for the event and, like his son, seemed miraculously to have hardly an ounce of fat on him.

— • —

We piled our rucksacks into a rickety old minibus, ready to embark on the six-hour drive to the mountains – but while we were refuelling the old vehicle, the brakes locked up. We were forced to hole up for an hour while they were being fixed, so I decided to take the team into a restaurant for a beer.

Seated round a couple of plastic tables that had seen better days, I asked everyone to introduce themselves and talk about their hopes and fears for the event. Be as candid as possible, I said. Most were concerned with how they would cope with the heavy loads in their rucksacks in the extreme heat: would they be the one to let the team down in the mountain?

When it came to my turn, I told them that I had concerns about the serious nature of this expedition. Primarily, the distance and height that we were undertaking with weight and heat, in more or less uncharted territory. If one person got into serious difficulty on the mountain, we might not be able to get them back to safety in time to save them. Every one of us had to sign up to this possibility,

I said. It was imperative that everyone had the courage to speak up if they were really suffering.

Finally, we all had to accept that there was a remote chance that we might not be able to make it up the mountain. We couldn't afford to drive one person into the ground for a shot at success, as that could put the whole team in jeopardy – if anyone collapsed or was seriously hurt, it would take all the efforts of the team to get them back alive.

— • —

We approached our would-be base camp in the dark. After a long and bumpy journey, we were relieved to spill out of the dusty vehicle and set up camp. One of the joys of sleeping out in the wilderness in Namibia is that it is dry and there is very little wind, so you can pretty much just roll your sleeping bag out on the ground and you're good to go.

That night, we feasted on giant steaks and chips made by Kobus on an open fire. The meal had the feel of a last supper about it, but it was a welcome one, as we knew that meals in the days ahead were going to be boil-in-a-bag ones.

The next morning, we awoke to find our sleeping bags damp from a cold sea mist. This was a welcome start to the day; the sun would soon be up to dry us out, so we packed quickly to get a start on it.

We would each be carrying three gallons of water, plus food. Just picking up our bags was almost impossible. They now weighed 75 pounds, more than the under-the-counter fridge that I'd purchased back home the week before. We would be climbing with fridges on our back. I felt like Sisyphus condemned to push his boulder uphill.

— • —

For the first few hours, I was amazed at how comfortable and robust the rucksacks felt. This isn't so bad, I thought. Then, the sun came up. In no time at all, the sheltered valley was an inferno. We had trained with heavy loads, but that preparation now felt woefully inadequate: quickly every step felt like a trial; boulders that should have been easy to scramble over felt twice as high. Though I remembered the pain of last year's expedition, had it really been this hard?

Although some of the team were also looking shocked, I was struggling to keep up with Kobus and the front runners. I started to feel a sense of inner panic as all my coping strategies went out the window. What if I ended up letting the team down? Had I bitten off more than I could chew this time? We took a break, but soon we were at it again, the pace as relentless as before.

We pressed on higher and higher through the boulders and rubble of the gorge and were just about to stop for a rest in the shade when one of the team, Tony, slipped on a loose rock. There was a crack as his ankle twisted and gave way. Our team medic, who we'd quickly taken to calling "The Doc", bound up Tony's injured ankle, but the swelling was already evident. He started to walk on it again but it was clear that, with four days of hard trekking ahead of us, he was never going to make it.

It was a crushing blow to lose someone, especially so early in the expedition, but, if it was going to happen, now was the best time. We were less than half a day into the trek and Kobus had invited two local guys to carry emergency water for the early stages of the climb, who now volunteered to take Tony back to base camp.

We were relieved to hear that evening on the satellite phone that he had made it down and was heading home to safety; he must have shown a lot of courage on that descent with what was subsequently diagnosed as a double-fractured ankle.

— • —

My friend and guide, Kobus, looks out onto the desert
from the Brandberg mountains, Namibia.

That night, I lay back and stared at the incredible starlit sky, which is probably one of the most wonderful treats of the Namibian wilderness. It was a joy to be able to rest in the cool, but now I was worried about The Doc. He'd patched Tony up OK, but I'd noticed that he'd been fading all afternoon. As we made camp that night, he admitted that he was suffering from diarrhoea and vomiting.

Despite injecting himself with an anti-sickness formula, he'd still struggled to hold down the evening meal. With the loads on our back, we should have been eating 7,000 calories a day. I doubted any of us were eating a third of that in this heat, but The Doc's luck needed to change if he was going to be strong enough for tomorrow.

At first light we were on our way. Kobus cranked up the pace and the sun grew stronger. By midday, we had crested the lip of the ridge onto the plateau – the Brandberg Mountains have a dome-like shape that makes it feel as if you could be walking over the back of a sleeping dinosaur. The plateau proved to be as tough going as the rocks the previous day.

The claw of panic returned. I gradually slipped to the back of the queue as the rest of the team overtook me one by one. I could see by the way that the guys were looking at me that they knew I was in trouble.

It never ceases to amaze me how instantly debilitating extreme heat can be. Anyone who has been to Bikram Yoga will tell you how, by the end of your first session in a superheated gym, all you want to do is get out of the room. In fact, they tell you on your first session that your goal is not to do the more difficult moves but simply to "stay in the room".

That thought had been occurring to me all morning. I had hoped that the plateau would be easier going, but it was strewn with row upon row of small rocky ridges, requiring you to do endless step-ups, while the packs still weighed a ton. I was desperate to sit down and rest… to get out of the room as quickly as possible. It was only the knowledge that I, the expedition leader, was holding up progress that kept me going forward.

The sun was high in the sky and beating down on us. Kobus found an undercut rocky cave, big enough to shelter us all, and called a halt for a three-hour break. He then helped The Doc to administer a drip to himself.

It reminded me of an incident during the Marathon De Sables where I had seen a runner during the race who was lying across the track being administered a drip by medics. That's him out of it then, I'd thought as I passed him. But half an hour later, the man passed me at a run and never looked back.

I was relieved to see, after an hour or so, The Doc looking similarly revived.

But The Doc, himself resurrected, was worried about Charles, who was fading to an ominous grey. He decided it was his turn for a drip while we sheltered from the worst of the sun. I started to think that if Charles was dehydrated then perhaps that was what was holding me back too. I had been keeping water back for emergencies, so I made a conscious effort to drink and eat plenty as we rested.

— • —

From the moment that we left the cave, John Whalley decided to stick with me for the rest of the day. Big John had been to the North Pole with me some years earlier and had been a stalwart of a previous expedition to Namibia. We trained in the same local gym and I knew that he could do more push-ups while in a handstand than I could manage the old-fashioned way.

As the terrain got steeper and rockier, he pulled me up some of the inclines, despite carrying not only his own kit but quite a bit of the weight from The Doc's kit too. His pack must have weighed more than 90 pounds, but he never said a word about it.

With one final slope to go before we broke for camp that day, I told the front runners to go on while The Doc – the elixir of his drip having now worn off – and I, would follow on slowly. Joakim, too, held back and offered to take The Doc's pack for him in 100-metre stretches up the hill. He would then come back down to get his own and catch us up. This was a heroic gesture and I could see that it was really tiring him out.

I had learnt the night before that Joakim's start in life had been a tough one. As a child, he'd had severe asthma and a number of serious allergic reactions that had seen him rushed to hospital. His father Borje had told me over the campfire, with tears in his eyes, how for a long time he hadn't dared imagine that Joakim would live beyond his early teenage years. Borje was immensely fond and proud of him, and I could see why.

Kobus came down to hike the last section with me.

"Don't be disillusioned when you get to the top," he said, "as there's still another ridge beyond it that we have to cross."

But I didn't care; that would be tomorrow's problem.

However, by the next day, we had decided that the state of the team and our dwindling water supplies meant that we would never make the summit. Instead, we would spend a day crossing the plateau in order to head directly for the nearest water hole on the other side, which we hoped would be at the start of the Hungarob Gorge, if it hadn't dried up.

All that day, I stuck to Kobus's heels, determined never to drop back. Big John had kindly taken a bit of my spare food, adding to his already heavy load, and my water supplies were down to a gallon or so after three days on the move. I now seemed to be back in a world that I could manage. That night – which would be our final night on the rock – we celebrated Charles' birthday around the campfire. It was great to see the team still laughing and Charles now with a whisky flask in his hand and big smile on face, having been on an intravenous drip only a day before.

— • —

The final stage was a precipitous rocky descent through the gorge. We came upon a watering hole not far from where we had expected to, but it looked stale and unfit for drinking. We pushed on, eventually coming across a clear pool further on.

We were in a jubilant mood as we filled our bottles and started to relax, when The Doc, bending down on a low ledge to fill up his water bottle, tumbled over the edge into the pool – what a place to have drowned!

Kobus and I were ahead of the rest of the team as we descended the rocky track from the watering hole, when I saw a dark crimson patch on the track in front of us and red paw marks. An animal had been killed here, and not too long ago. Two more of the team crossed the blood patch but the third person, Mark, stopped and bent over to do up his boot, as a five-foot-long, dappled coat shot out across the track in front of him and raced up the rock.

Startled, he yelled out that he'd just seen a leopard. Coming back up the slope, Kobus found it hard to believe him – he'd only ever seen two leopards in the Brandberg Mountains in all his life. But as he looked over the bloody tracks, he concluded that the leopard must have been crouched in the small cave, no more than a metre to the left of the track where he and I had passed by.

The only time that leopards attack is when they are disturbed when eating or cornered, he said. Had we stopped to examine the blood and caught its eye in such close proximity, there's a good chance it could have gone for us. As it was, it must have seen its chance to make a break for it when Mark provided a gap in our passage.

A lucky escape for us all, particularly as Kobus told me that a leopard's preferred method of attack is to jump up and dig its teeth and front claws into your head, while the bunched up rear claws rip your stomach and intestines out.

It was a relief, when, at around five o'clock in the evening, we finally made it down to the bottom of the valley. Kobus drew a mark in the sand with his boot and welcomed us, one by one, over the finishing line.

— • —

Though a short expedition compared to many that I had undertaken before, those four days on the sun-baked rock had been among the hardest, and potentially most dangerous, that I had ever endured. As I returned home to the Essex countryside, I had to ask myself why, in my late 60s, I was still putting myself on the line in wild and inhospitable places.

The most honest answer is the simplest one: I still enjoy it. The nights in the desert are long, peaceful and beautiful, and out there, all that I have to think about is the simple task in front of me – often, literally putting one foot in front of the other – to get myself and my team to the top and back in one piece.

All the time when involved in such adventures I am conscious constantly of the price of failure, which can be death. And though this can be a sobering thought at times, it can serve to focus the mind. Never am I more in touch with reality than when facing some severe ordeal in the outdoors, and maybe this is partly the attraction of such a life – the rest of life's problems shrink into obscurity and I understand what it is to be truly present in the moment.

To come home from an adventure is also always a joy. I return to the same place, to the people I love, refreshed and, hopefully, a bit wiser, more humble, grateful.

So, these days, while I feel more like a lumbering old bear than the climber, runner or rower I was when I wore a younger man's clothes, I still find peace in acts of adventure. And I know that this particular bear can stand and look out to sea, knowing the sea. He can look up at the mountains that a young boy once dreamed of climbing and know that some of his soul will rest there.

And that same old bear knows that it is in those places that seem so threatening from the outside that you find beauty, benevolence and inspiration.

TWENTY-ONE

A Dream Of White Horses

"He who goes slow, he goes good, he goes far."

Old mountaineering guide's proverb

I f I think back on past expeditions – certainly when I think of the really big ones to the Himalayas or the Atlantic crossing – they were a great escape for me, whether it was from running the police station, the business feeling stuck in a rut, troubled relationships or pressures at home. The moment that I stepped onto that plane, train or boat that would transport me to a far-off land, I was free. Free, but never alone. After all, how much fun can a tough, arduous experience be when you're on your own? I always chose camaraderie over competition, and still do.

One memory from 1986 stands out. We had just selected the team for the Himalayas and I remember countless late nights in the office having to deal with endless piles of admin that were mounting up in preparation for the expedition.

The rest of the team's job was simply to keep fit and get in as much climbing as possible without getting injured. One of our best climbers then was a detective constable called Gordon Briggs. He was in his late 20s and had a natural, easy talent on the rock face, and since he worked in the same geographic area as me, we would occasionally bump into each other.

We got talking about climbs that we had done and I confessed that, having nearly always been the one to lead as a young man, and having never been properly schooled in rock climbing, I'd only rarely climbed routes graded "severe". Gordon, by contrast, climbed regularly at "very severe" or "extreme". He offered to take me up to North Wales to get some good routes in on the rocks, and I jumped at the chance.

After spending the night at an old friend's house in Bangor, Gordon and I made for Anglesey to climb some sea cliffs at a well-known spot called Gogarth. Our target was to be the tantalisingly named A Dream of White Horses, a climb consisting of a long traverse some 150 feet above the sea. For the most part, it followed a series of thin cracks in the rock and aside from being extremely difficult, its attractions included stunning views out to sea, an exhilarating feeling of being totally exposed to the elements and the rhythmic sound of the waves crashing against the rocks far below – a constant reminder of what awaited you should you fall.

We anchored onto a rock at the highest point of the climb and Gordon started to edge out left along the traverse, seasoned hands feeling for holds. For relatively inexperienced climbers like myself, the waiting is the most nerve-wracking part. Once I get on the rock and start moving, I always feel much better.

Gordon, who clearly had no such nerves, had already covered half the distance to his destination and was busy jamming a small runner into a vertical crack in the rock. He clipped a carabiner on to this and ran the rope through it so that it spooled out loosely behind him. This was standard practice for climbers. As long as I was holding the rope securely at my end, Gordon could continue his traverse, safe in the knowledge that if he fell, he would pendulum on the runner and be able to clamber back up.

Unfortunately, I had decided to give the rope a flick to free up a kink in the line. This flick was more violent than I intended and I watched in horror as Gordon's life-saving runner came loose of its crack and slid down the rope towards me.

"Should I tell him?" I thought. "Or would it be better if he climbed on innocence?"

But while my mind was wrestling with the decision, some other part of me had started to laugh. That kind of nervous, unhinged laughter that sometimes bubbles up when a situation feels almost too serious to be tolerable.

Gordon had heard me and turned to look back. I thought he would holler abuse at me when he realised what had happened, but instead he just stood there with a smirk on his face.

"I don't know what you're laughing at," he said. "Now you're going to have to follow me across the whole length of this traverse with no protection. That will be fun for you!"

Once Gordon was tied to his belay position, I moved off nervously, terrified of what would be a long and potentially fatal drop if I missed my footing. It felt like an eternity before I reached his position. This wasn't helped by his constant big grin and stream of ribald comments. Nevertheless, I had made it, to my relief.

A grinning Gordon Briggs on A Dream of White Horses in Anglesey, North Wales,
just before I inadvertently flicked his runner out of the rock face.

From here, the final pitch involved a short traverse across a rather
messy patch of rocks and then a climb up to the finish. Gordon
decided that it was my turn to lead and, with new-found confidence
that the worst might be over, I set off up what should have been quite
a straightforward finish to the route.

In my ignorance, I climbed too high, too early and ended up off-route; the holds thinned out and, with some alarm, I realised that I was in trouble again.

On the way up, I had managed to put in a runner, but I wasn't at all confident now that it would hold a fall. I reached, or rather lunged, for a flake of rock high up to my left… and it peeled away in my hands.

There was a split-second where I found myself looking at the rock in my hands, then I lost my balance; my feet slipping off the tiny holds they were on, my body plummeting down the rock face, heading for the sea.

Miraculously, the runner held. I came to a stop with a jolt, breathing hard. I clumsily swung back onto the rock and clambered up to the top of the climb, amid hoots of derision from my friend, who, on seeing that I was OK, now wasted no time in putting the boot in.

As we drove back to Bangor from the climb, Gordon put on *Wish You Were Here* by Pink Floyd. It was a beautiful sunlit evening, and even though I had realised that I would probably never make a really good rock climber – I just didn't seem to have the natural feel for it that true climbers like Gordon did – I felt elated.

So moved was I by that song after a fantastic adventure with a good buddy, and the camaraderie that comes with shared endeavour, that, even now, when I hear that song the hairs stand up on the back of my neck.

Epilogue

"In the cave you fear to enter lies the treasure you seek."

Joseph Campbell

For all the time that I've spent going on adventures, I've invested just as much time in trying to work out what drives people like me to seek them out in the first place. I found part of the answer in the work of Joseph Campbell, whose book, *The Hero with a Thousand Faces*, explores the theory that all of our important myths share a fundamental structure – the hero's journey.

In Campbell's theory, the hero begins life in an ordinary world, but soon hears a call to adventure, whereupon he senses that he must leave and journey to a far-off land. His journey tests him to the point of collapse many times, though he often succeeds because of help he has earned along the way from someone older or wiser. Eventually, the hero finds the "treasure" and, if he can succeed in returning to the normal world, finds that he is transformed.

My aim in writing this book has been to tell the stories of my adventures in the most honest way that I can – warts and all. In most of the accounts, far from being "a hero on a journey", I often stumble through the briar in new and unfamiliar territories, trying to find a path towards survival or success. But I believe this journey replicates the pathway for most of us in our lives in one way or another. The treasure for me is a store of experience, learning and research that has, over time, helped me understand how to take the kernel of a seemingly-impossible idea and make it a reality.

At 70 years old, much of my life is now spent helping other adventurers find success in their own endeavours. I work with individuals, couples and teams who are setting out on serious, and sometimes potentially dangerous, journeys, where the possibility of safe return is not always certain.

It is a privileged position to be in and one that I do not take lightly. For all of us, I believe that if we do not build up the courage to leave our comfort zones and enter the cave, we will never find that elusive treasure. May your journey bring you the fulfilment that you deserve.

Acknowledgements

True adventures are often only made possible by the support of others. So it has been the case for this book. It has taken several years to write and only with the support and patience of some very good people.

Early attempts involved tons of handwritten notes that were then laboriously transcribed by my sons Chris and Julian, and Jill Moeser. Jo Clarke worked on some early scripts as well as my good friend Jonathan Blain, who kept me inspired and energised when my spirits were flagging.

My buddy Big John Whalley generously lent me his house in Mallorca for a couple of weeks to write in peace, which gave me my first big breakthrough and enabled me to get 40,000 words or so down on paper.

The one person who really stepped up to the mark and made the book come alive was a good friend of my sons, George Bull. George writes for a living and is also a good long distance runner himself. He offered to pull the mound of papers together into one coherent document and help get it published.

He is a joy to work with as he has the same fascination with endurance as myself. Our planning meetings were always inspiring and stimulating, and I am indebted to him for his support and understanding throughout this project, which has spanned a number of years.

My fellow adventurers are too many to mention. So please, if you're reading this book, forgive me if I have left you out, but know that I'll always be grateful for the time that we spent together in those far-flung places.

There are some people that I must mention, without whose generous sponsorship some of my most recent expeditions might never have been possible: John Whalley, Jim Wilkinson, Mark White and Peter Swift. We've shared some good adventures and survived some close shaves.

My thanks also to Professor Lew Hardy, who has guided me on a number of mountaineering expeditions and without whom we might never have gone to the Himalayas – or certainly not have come back alive. He has taught me some vital coping strategies for surviving and thriving in dangerous and stressful situations.

My two sons – Chris and Julian – have joined me on expeditions and have been great companions along the way. As has my oldest son, Marcus, who came with me as expedition doctor to Kyrgyzstan a few years ago and deftly sewed my thumb back on near the summit of a mountain.

Another person who deserves a special mention is Fraser Dodds. A longstanding companion on a number of early adventures, Fraser was the one person who was courageous enough (or mad enough) to join me on our epic row across the Atlantic Ocean. He is a giant of a man in every sense of the word and has an equally big heart.

When I told a seasoned ocean rower that I was considering rowing in a pair, he warned me that the greatest danger I would come across wouldn't be the storms, giant tankers or sharks, but that at some point, I would want to kill my rowing partner and he would want to kill me.

"The only thing that will stop you," he said, "is the thought of being found out."

Well, Fraser and I still remain the closest of friends and if I were ever to be in a tight spot, whether on land or out to sea, Fraser would be the person that I would choose to stand beside me.

Thanks also to Kenneth and Tatiana Crutchlow from the Ocean Rowing Society for giving me the initial confidence and knowledge to even consider rowing across the Atlantic, and to Phil Scantlebury for racing out on a yacht to capture Fraser and me as we overshot Barbados in our boat.

Finally, I am indebted to my family and friends, who have stood beside me throughout a lifetime of adventure. Among these friends, I particularly want to mention John and Libby Robertson, who stood by Elaine when I was away on some of the more perilous expeditions. John has also joined me on many adventures himself, including the first British ascent of Jogin 1, and has always been a loyal and supportive friend.

The toughest task for anyone left behind is that of waiting for people to return. This courageous task has invariably fallen to my wife, Elaine. She has been the one who has cried alone at night sometimes, wondering if I might ever return. She has also been the one who was left alone for weeks on end dealing with three growing boys.

What I expected of her was far from fair and reasonable at times. She was, and will always be, my rock and my base camp, and has got me out of many a scrape when I was stuck for ideas in the middle of nowhere. I am forever indebted to her. She has my love and deepest gratitude forever.

J.P.
Bantham, August 2015

The Author

John Peck is a former 2nd Lieutenant in the 1st Battalion, Staffordshire Regiment, where he was a member of a successful British Army expedition to Mt. Popocatépetl in Mexico in 1966. On leaving the army, he joined the Metropolitan Police Service as a constable patrolling the streets of London. Before long, he found himself commanding a police division in Stoke Newington, then a notoriously dangerous part of the city, throughout the riots of the mid-1980s.

He has always pushed himself to do extraordinary things. In 1986, he led a British/Indian police expedition to summit unclimbed peaks in the Himalayas. He learned much about leadership during this period and was invited to run leadership development programmes for senior police officers at the National Police Staff College in Hampshire.

In 1995, at the age of 50, he was starting to get restless and left the police service to set up his own consultancy, training business leaders in the private sector.

In 2004, John became the oldest British person to row across the Atlantic unsupported and spent the next decade seeing how his body and mind could cope in extreme situations, from serial desert marathons to walking to the North Pole.

At the time of writing, John splits his time between coaching senior business managers through his consultancy, Tiger Teams, and running wilderness survival programmes on remote Scottish islands for inner-city youth leaders working with violent gangs. He is well known for his powerful talks in which he inspires people to take on challenges in their own lives that may at first seem impossible – a subject dear to his heart.

Much of this work he does with his wife Elaine and his three sons – all of whom have been with him on expeditions over the years. He lives in Essex.

To find out more about John's work, go to
www.restlessthebook.co.uk

Printed in Great Britain
by Amazon